# Radically Unfinished

ONE WOMAN'S PROJECT TO FIND AUTHENTIC, UNCOMPLICATED CONFIDENCE

Erin Fischer
CEO and Owner,
The Leadership and Training Studio

Edition 1
Productivity Studio, LLC
2017

**Radically Unfinished**
**One Woman's Project to Find Authentic, Uncomplicated Confidence**



Published by Productivity Studio, LLC
Cover Design by Danielle Groves
Text Layout by Danielle Groves
Edited by Aileen Toomey
Reviewed by Sophia Longest
Title inspiration from Danielle Geary

To order books or inquire about bulk sales:
www.theleadershipandtrainingstudio.com

Distributed by:
The Leadership and Training Studio, LLC

Library of Congress Control Number: 2016963484
Library of Congress Cataloging-in-Publication Data
Fischer, Erin
Radically Unfinished
One Woman's Project to Find Authentic, Uncomplicated Confidence
ISBN: 978-0-692-82657-7

1. Education

Printed in the United States of America

# dedication

To the brave, bold women who have helped shape my journey.

# a big reminder

I have been drawn to this topic for years, and I am honored to share my journey with you. My hope is that you use your new knowledge on authentic confidence, but also you pass it on to other women in your life who need authentic confidence, too. Please, I beg you, don't let this topic rest just with you in your own space. Talk about it, debate it, ruminate on it, let it rattle in your brain, and then, pay it forward. Help another woman find her authentic confidence so she can do more in this world that she ever imagined.

# my lens

I wrote this book for all women, but I want to share that my lens impacts my confidence. You see, my lens is being a speaker, a traveler, a former camp director, a lover of non-profit work, a kid friendly aunt with no kids, and a woman who has collected stories from over 21,000 people in my audiences. As you read, I implore you to use your own lens so you can find your stories, and your own pattern to authentic confidence.

# foreword

If I am being transparent, this book could have been easily called *Confidence For Shy, Introverted, Quiet, No-Need-To-Be-The-Center-Of-Attention Women*. The irony is not lost on me. I am not a natural when it comes to confidence, much like my current shade of brunette. My wisdom does not come from excellence, but from hard work and relentless practice. It's like being an Olympian, except there isn't a panel of patriots to judge the sport of confidence. Rather, I have a very tough, internal judge that can be relentless. As my friend Heather recently reminded me, "It's what we tell ourselves that can be so encouraging or so damaging."

As a matter of fact, as I write this book, I step back and laugh. Why on earth am I writing this charge on this topic? I glare at myself, not for being ambitious, but for being bold enough to write about a topic that I must consciously and consistently practice each and every moment of my day.

If you knew me, it would be clear to you that I live in this space of being daring, courageous, intrepid, and audacious mixed perfectly with a feeling of being reserved, overly thoughtful and concerned, people pleasing, quiet and restrained. But, I realized and have become insanely certain that the vast majority of us live in that space, too. It's the third space - the place right in between two extremes. It's the middle of excited and scared, nervous and happy, and all in and all out. I have found that I am in the middle of confidence. Some days it is easy and some days difficult, some days natural and some days forced, and some days motivating and some days daunting.

With absolute certainty, I am no expert in being authentically confident, yet I have such a strong pull to this topic. It is like a magnet in my life – even when I am tired of it, want to let it go, want to repel it – there it is staring me down. It is a force stronger than nearly any other force in my life. Furthermore, it's because I have met so many talented, brave and purpose-driven women who are holding back for a million reasons and also one. This one reason is lack of confidence. I wrote this book to honor their path, too.

With this force so strong, I was encouraged to write my stories. These stories are the true stories of my own journey.

# table of contents

# Section One:
# First Things First

# first things first

# 1.1

## MY WHY

**DON'T SKIP THIS PART!** I am always guilty of two things when I read. I skip the introduction, (what a waste to time, let me get to the good stuff) and I read the last page of every book, first. But this time, I must stop you for a minute to tell you why this work is so important.

To begin, I am fascinated by human behavior, and I am curious about my own habits in and around confidence. Believe it or not, I wrote a different version of this book once before, and learned so much writing *The Freshman Project* that I started from scratch, again. This book is two and a half years in the making, and came from my own inquisitiveness and years of interactions with incredible women who saw me keynote on confidence. They were brave enough to share their own stories during and after my talks.

Along the way, out on the road, I had a profound 'aha' moment. I thought it was just the college women that I serve who needed to learn about confidence, and then I realized that it is women of all ages. They, too, were stopping me to speak about their struggles. Women who add the intersectionality of race, religion, gender and sexual preference shared the additional layers to unfold. They taught me to keep my eyes wide open when I am in the pursuit of championing confidence for all women.

What I learned along the way is that women are a lot like old, beautiful houses – the ones we buy on HGTV with all of the charm and character. The homes with multiple shades of gray and chic curtains - but inside many of them are suffering. It's the pipes, the electrical work, the roof and everything else in between. These women seem to have it all together, but when asked how they are really doing, they share that they suffer from anxiety and depression, feel like impostors, feel inadequate, are preferring perfection over growth, and so much more. They are sitting silently - so fearful that the real version will be too much for someone else. So, they hide it and don't name it or own it, and I want that to stop.

"They are sitting silently - so fearful that the real version will be too much for someone else. So, they hide it and don't name it or own it, and I want that to stop."

So, I started writing. This book is a collection of my stories because I know I can't give advice on how to be authentically confident without first finding my own strength. Plus, I know that giving advice is overrated. I want to honor that every woman I meet is an individual with her own story and her own path to confidence. This book is a guide to how I found my place, with one hope attached to it. My goal is that through my stories, you see yourself somewhere and decide what your confidence pattern is.

Just like solving math problems, or fixing a flat tire, there is a pattern and a cadence to how we work as humans. As you begin to read, take notes and figure out what you can add to make this personal for you. Find the pattern in all of it so that when you get stuck again, you have a place to start.

first things first

# 1.2

# THE SOAPBOX AND FORT WAYNE TRAIN

**THIS IS THE STORY OF HOW I GOT STARTED.** There were a few things I had to do before I got to the hard work. First I wanted to take ownership for the reason why I started all this work for women. Plus, I wanted to uncover my personal bias around confidence, including studying my myths and truths. I needed to figure out how I got here, in the first place.

I made a simple decision. I was going to get on my soapbox for about three minutes. I was standing in a beautiful, well-appointed lecture hall with three hundred collegiate women staring at me, and they were not saying a word.

How was this possible? Literally, how could a massive hall full of women be so well behaved, quiet and unobtrusive in a large space that screams: Discuss, debate, and use your voice to learn!

I was on a gorgeous college campus as a volunteer for a national organization and it was a remarkable Saturday afternoon. Three hundred women were giving up four hours to learn about goal setting for their organization.

But, I kept wondering, "Why are they not engaging?" Why are they not speaking up? I knew from my initial interaction and planning meetings that these women were smart, clever and social? They shared with me that they were excited for this program and they told me about what an involved group of women they were.

Finally, after three arduous hours, I stopped asking questions and jumped up on my imaginary, but very sizable soapbox.

I said to them, "I have to stop all of this for a quick moment." This was not something I would normally do; this was far from the norm of what you are taught as a professional speaker or facilitator. However, I continued, "I am going to get up on my soapbox for just a second. I have traveled a fair distance to be with all of you today, and given up a free weekend away from home. I am dying to hear what you have to say. Yet, when I ask you a question, you share your response with a partner and talk for quite some time, but the minute I ask you to share your response with the group, it is silent." I used a pregnant pause for a bit of drama.

"Why?," I explored. Then, I went "academic" on them for a minute and briefly described the Impostor Phenomenon.

The research from Dr. Pauline Rose Clance shows that women believe their success is created on the basis of luck - not hard work. As a result, many women have developed these habits of not believing in themselves. For instance, they don't raise their hand when they are in a classroom or a boardroom, they don't sit in the front of the room at a meeting, they don't offer their voice and, sadly, they think they are frauds and impostors.

Was I experiencing this right now? Were these intelligent women really afraid to share their voice? When I stepped down from my faux box, I said to them, "Thanks for letting me have that moment." It was a bit odd for me as a volunteer to be so brazen while talking to a group of women I would never see again, but my gut told me that I had to say something. There were several different things that could be at play, and I was fully aware of that. After all, it was Saturday afternoon, and we were talking about goals. It's not exactly glamorous all the time.

As I finished sharing my bit of advice with the women, they finally started talking, and now I couldn't get them to stop. I was reveling in this chatter.

For me, there is nothing better than having to stop a conversation, due to time, because it is so thoughtful and interactive. They started to share with me that they were afraid to raise their hands, but most importantly why they were terrified of being wrong in front of others. They would rather listen and not know the answer than share or guess incorrectly in front of 300 "friends."

> "They would rather listen and not know the answer than share or guess the wrong thing in front of 300 'friends.'"

Now, my mind was moving a mile a minute. I wanted them to be wrong! I wanted them to be really wrong and be okay with it, but I only had an hour left and a lot of curriculum to get through. I was happy they were engaging, but I felt like I had to keep moving forward. Instead, they thoughtfully kept sharing. They said that it is hard to speak up in big lecture halls, and there is a true fear about being too bold or too confident. After hearing this, I was not so thrilled. This confirmed what I discovered in my research on authentic confidence for women. I was there to facilitate conversations about priorities and goals, but my mind was stuck on these women's inability to speak up in front of others, and the great impact it was having on their lives.

I thought about this for days after. Maybe it was their confidence, their southern hospitality or the norms they had created within their group. Whatever it was, I was curious, and I wanted to know why these women were not speaking up, even when the expectation from me was clear, at the beginning. What was at the core of their disadvantage? Where did they learn that you are either right, or you don't say a word.

Then, I remembered. I am a member of this group of women – not these 300 – but a larger group of women who opt out. I have felt like an impostor myself. So, as I sat on the plane ride home, I started thinking about how I went from a shy, sweet kid to a speaker who dances with my audience on stage.

For me, I distinctly remember a time when I was at the Children's Zoo in my hometown. One of the best things to do was get on the Zoo train after you had seen all of the animals and been accosted at the goat feeding exhibit. By the way, no one allows their kids to cross the street these days, but in the 80s it was perfectly acceptable to allow young children to traverse through a pen with 30 goats and let the goats jump on you as you sat helplessly in your stroller trying to feed them little pellets of disgusting, grainy food.

After being accosted, the reward was this magical train ride, and it was not like a regular zoo train that went around in a little circle and brought you back in two minutes. No, this train was pretty splendid for our hometown. You would jump on and ride out into the woods past this beautiful swan and duck filled lake and make a big U-turn and head back through this classic train tunnel. We took the train ride nearly every time we went to the zoo, but on this occasion, my mom's friend Theresa was with us. Simply stated, she was fun. She was not crazy fun, but she was cool and beautiful,l and she seemed to have a lot of confidence from my young vantage point. As we were getting on the train she asked the conductor, "Can we sit in the front – the very front where we can see it all?" Without blinking an eye, the conductor said, "Yes."

She quickly looked at me, the oldest of the three, and said, "Erin, do you want to come up here with us?" I looked at my mom with a huge sigh, looked back at my mom's friend, and then looked at my mom one last time and quietly said, "No." Then, I sat on that long train ride, riddled with regret. Not the kind of regret you feel after getting in trouble because you were mean to your little brother, or the kind of regret you feel from picking the wrong ice cream at Baskin Robbins – the gumball ice cream was always a poor life choice. This was real regret. We were all going to the same place, but my train ride was not nearly as interesting as the ride my mom's friend and her two girls were having. Even as a little kid, I felt so disappointed.

I have thought about that train ride a lot lately. It must have been one of those life-defining moments. The kind that you don't know is happening to you, but as soon as it does, you know it will stick with you. That is and will be the foundation memory of my lack of confidence. I wish this was the only thing on my list, but it is just the starting point of a long list of regrets of not trying something, jumping in, exploring fully, or being presently confident. It's easy to be confident with a long distance, far off decision. It is even easier when you have hindsight and can look back at a decision you can easily do over in your mind. My bright orange pumpkin Halloween costume at 11 years old – that's an easy do over.

Right now, being presently confident is my new, daily homework. It means being intentional, thoughtful, in-the-moment, and consciously confident. It means that I am in the practice of choosing confidence just like I choose which shoes to wear. I have to choose confidence just like I choose almonds over snack cakes. I have to choose confidence just like I choose exercise over an afternoon nap – even though I secretly think both have their merits. I have to choose confidence like I choose other things, like kindness when I am tired, boldness when I am on stage, or even patience when I am traveling. One is much easier than the other, but it's my goal to be aware of my confidence and, in turn, begin to influence and reframe it. I want it to move from haphazardly hoping it will happen – like losing holiday weight – and move toward a stream of awareness around my own choices.

I want to be mindful that sometimes I am the girl on the train or even the 300 women in the lecture hall, but being consciously confident is the plan.

## Consider this:

- What is your soapbox moment? When have you told others to be confident, knowing you should work on doing the same?

- When have you felt like an impostor? What did it feel like, and more importantly, what did you miss out on, as a result?

- What is your Fort Wayne Train story? What is your first memory of not being confident? What do you wish you could have done differently?

- How will this knowledge impact your confidence?

first things first

# 1.3

# THE MYTHS AND TRUTHS ABOUT CONFIDENCE

**I HAVE BEEN THINKING ABOUT CONFIDENCE WITH INTENTION FOR SEVEN YEARS -** as much as I think about brownies, my favorite holiday Christmas, whether my sweet Yorkie will live to be 16, or if I made a complete a total fool of myself on any given day. So, all the time! It's a persistent thought; my work on authentic confidence is always present and looking for its purpose.

Recently, I have begun thinking about my confidence in a different way. In doing so, I started to see a pattern, and more clearly, I started to see what is true for me about confidence. On the flip side, I also began to identify what was completely and utterly untrue, too – even though it is hard to be that brutally honest with myself. But, there was one hiccup.

If I "see" someone who is confident in any way, I think, 'they must be confident.' It's like a woman who can pull off mix-matched patterns from the J.Crew catalog. What I've found is that I've had confirmation bias all over the idea of confidence. (Confirmation bias is also called myside bias.) When I look for reassurance in a hectic world, I search for information that confirms my own assumptions. A great example is the craziness that has ensued during the 2016 elections. I can find confirmation of all of my values, feelings, and truths about my candidate without blinking an eye even while other truths exist. For instance, I have confirmed that my accountant is good because he asks a lot of questions. I have confirmed that my hairdresser is the best because it is hard to get onto her schedule, and I have confirmed that my vet is a rock star because he is sweet to my dog. I am always searching for these clues to tell me if something is true or not, but never considered that my clues might be really wrong, but as my friend Helen reminded me this year, being a critical thinker means I have to override confirmation bias for reality. I have to mind my blind spots and ask deeper and more thoughtful questions like, "Do I not agree with someone's idea because I don't like them?" My clues lead me to some bad assumptions about my own confidence – the hiccup.

"I have to mind my blind spots and ask deeper and more thoughtful questions like, 'Do I not agree with someone's idea because I don't like them?'"

I wanted to be sure that I really understood the concept of confidence, without all of my confirmation bias before I started to click on the right pattern. So, I jotted down notes about the truths and myths around confidence, and here is what I discovered:

MYTH 1 If you are tall, pretty, have money in your bank account, are exceptional at something important, live in the right apartment, and have tall and pretty friends, you have confidence.

MYTH 2 If you are naturally extroverted, outgoing, have a sense of humor and can make people laugh, you have confidence.

MYTH 3 If you are a risk taker, do brave things, like skydiving or going on a reality TV show, you have confidence.

MYTH 4 If you come from the perfect family, perfect background, or have the perfect education, you have confidence.

**MYTH 5** If you walk in the room like you own it, dress to the nines, and have your nothing in your teeth when you eat a salad, you have confidence.

**MYTH 6** If your parents, grandparents, aunts or uncles are or were confident, you are automatically confident, and more importantly if your parents, grandparents, aunts or uncles were not confident, then neither are you.

**MYTH 7** If you didn't arrive in this world naturally confident, then you are out of luck.

**MYTH 8** If you are not afraid of a damn thing, you have confidence.

**MYTH 9** If you have confidence, you have it all the time.

**THE TRUTH** I am always searching for authentic confidence. I wish I could have more of it, and I wish it would be way easier to find and keep it. The truth is that my confidence comes and goes. It can feel like catching a bubble in a windstorm. It is a skill to be mastered over a lifetime, not a place of arrival or a finish line.

The myth was that it would all come to me on some magical birthday, but it never arrived in a pretty package. I assumed it would get easier, which is partly true, but it is still an intentional action – a choice for me. The truth is that I have come to the realization that confidence, my confidence, will have to be at the top of my mind, and I will have to pick it like I am picking a partner or a career. I have to choose, with intent, to be consciously confident – every single day.

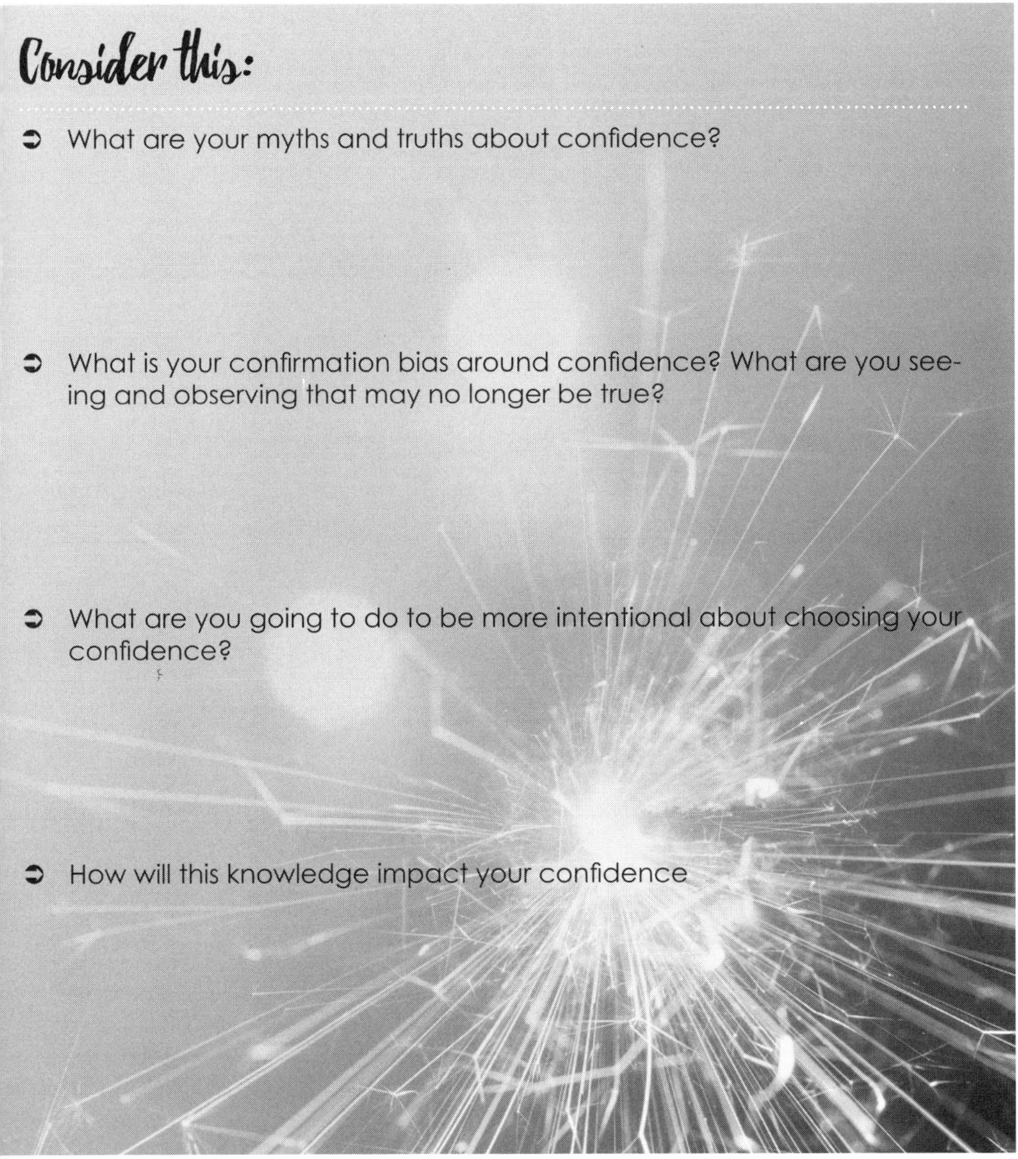

# Consider this:

- What are your myths and truths about confidence?

- What is your confirmation bias around confidence? What are you seeing and observing that may no longer be true?

- What are you going to do to be more intentional about choosing your confidence?

- How will this knowledge impact your confidence

first things first

# 1.4

# MY SEARCH AND SECRET OBSESSION

**I HAVE BEEN IN ROOMS WITH WOMEN WHO ARE OVERLY CONFIDENT AND ARROGANT,** and I have been in rooms with women who are painfully under confident and insecure. Both make my heart hurt. My search, however, is for this fine line in between. It feels like walking a tight rope some days, but my clarity comes in knowing what I am looking for: Authentic confidence.

> "The best way I know how to explain authentic confidence is this: It's knowing who you are, knowing who you are not, and unequivocally knowing the difference. It feels like a click into your own space, an exhale into ease, and a realization of alignment with your thoughts and actions."

The best way I know how to explain authentic confidence is this: It's knowing who you are, knowing who you are not, and unequivocally knowing the difference. It feels like a click into your own space, an exhale into ease, and a realization of alignment with your thoughts and actions.

For me, it's being in a room full of wonderful human beings and having the confidence to raise my hand when I can contribute, and equally and as confidently raise my hand and ask, "Can you tell me what you mean? I am lost here." It's walking into the room and firmly shaking the hand of the VIP, as well as helping the server with the boxes at the end of a party. It's asking for what I want, and also being willing to compromise. It's being an expert and a novice, and being an authority on a subject and an inquisitive learner on something I never knew existed.

I am not looking for a perfect game, match or even a perfect score, and when I get stuck, I keep thinking of those amazing women on the Olympic gymnastics squad. None of them got a perfect score, yet the US team won the gold medal. Quarterbacks get sacked and still get a win, CEOs put out a bad product every once in a while and still make the financial projections, parents lose their marbles sometimes and still produce kind, gentle souls. Perfection is not the plan when it comes to authentic confidence.

I am also looking for uncomplicated confidence. I don't need another job or more work. What I need is something easy, and still tailored made. I don't mind something a bit messy, or hard, but I don't want something so confusing that I end up quitting this work.

So, authentic and uncomplicated have become my posts. My hope is simple. I want to be on the search for a pattern that works for me, and I want to find people who support my growth for a more focused life. But first, with some encouragement, I decided to take an inventory of myself.

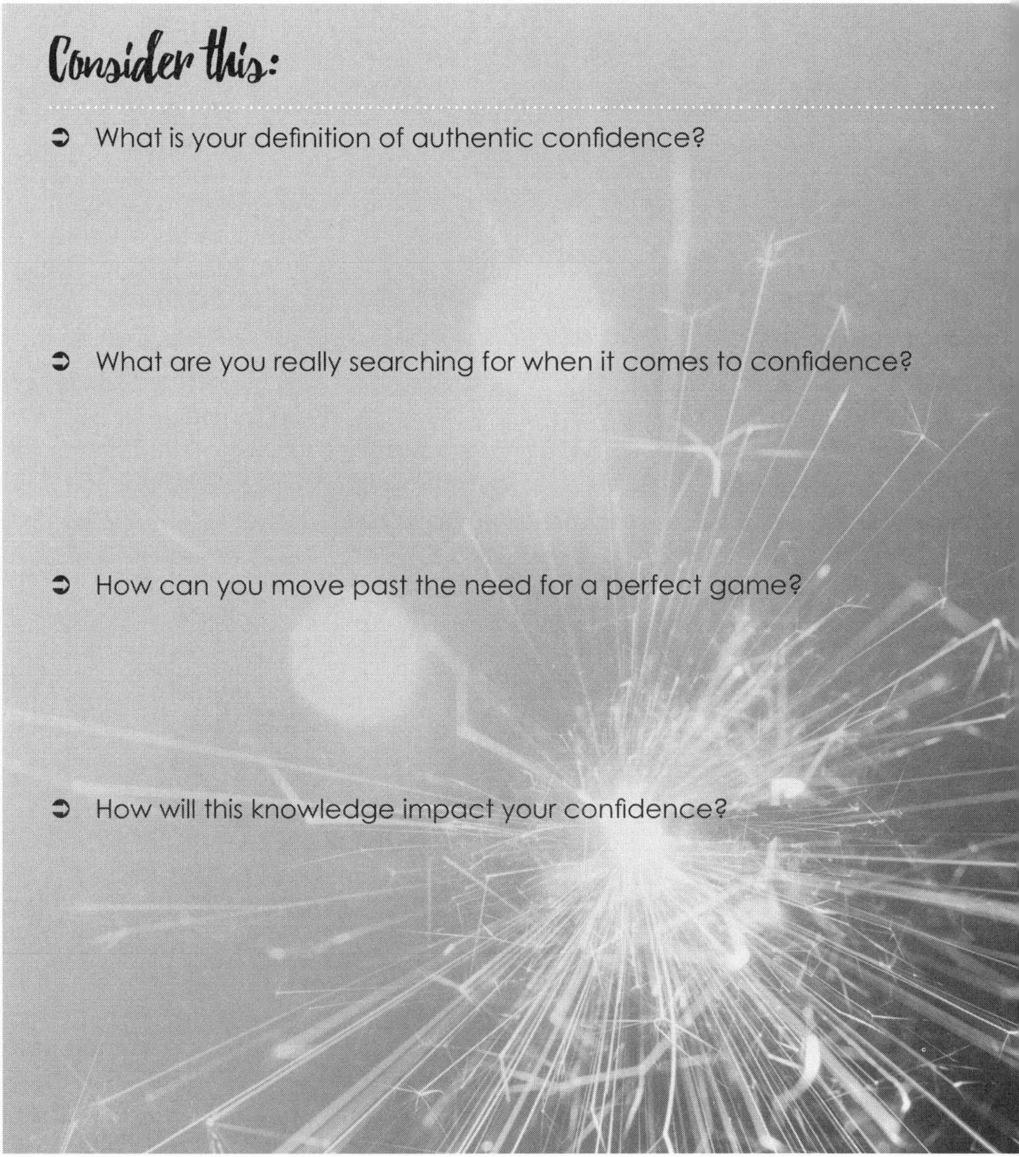

## Consider this:

- What is your definition of authentic confidence?

- What are you really searching for when it comes to confidence?

- How can you move past the need for a perfect game?

- How will this knowledge impact your confidence?

# 1.5

## NEVER HAVE I EVER

**NEVER HAVE I EVER SMOKED A CIGARETTE.** Lord, I have never TP'd a house, or keyed a car when I was mad, and I have never had the guts to throw a punch – even if someone deserved it. (Except for a boy named Marcus who I knocked down in the 4th grade. I literally forgot about that until today.) As I start to write this list, I have realized that I am a rule breaker - who follows most of all the rules.

There is a long list of things I will probably never do, but I also have an equally long list of things that I am afraid to do. There is a huge difference for me. I see confidence coming from a place of really knowing who I am and who I am not. I know what I am willing to do for a good time or a good story, but I have a hidden compartment in me that goes beyond a conscientious list of rights and wrongs. In this hidden compartment is another list of things that scare me.

Let's first start with what I am not afraid of these days. I am not afraid of bugs, roller coasters, skydiving, kids of any age, of getting in front of a group of 800 people during a keynote, and I am not afraid of a challenge or confrontation. I am not afraid to stand up to things I think are wrong. Ask the gentleman on the running trail behind my house. He was riding his bike and tethered to a leash was a beautiful dog running next to him.

It was too hot outside for that animal to be running that fast, and I was not afraid to tell that man how strongly I felt. So, being an engaged community member – not a problem.

Also, I am not afraid to send my food back if it is undercooked - much to my husband's dread. I am not afraid to be a super involved aunt to my nieces and nephews or to show love to the people who are incredibly important to me. I am not afraid of mistakes or even speaking up in staff meetings. I am not afraid of birthdays or getting older.

Now, I embrace a new birthday, joyfully. My husband's aunt said that each birthday brought a new sense of confidence for her and that she looked forward to big milestone birthdays. She is right – birthdays mean you have more experience under your belt and you are ready to take on new challenges. Despite this advice, turning 30 was unbearable. People talk about wanting to stop their babies from growing up, but I wanted to stop my 30th birthday. Logically, I knew it was impossible, but I had this strong, visceral feeling of wanting to somehow screech the brakes of a fast moving train.

Our friend John was the one who helped me with my 30th birthday. John and I are close friends – the kind of friends that know the best parts of one another and the not-so-great parts, too. My husband and I helped him through a tough divorce, and he is certainly like family to us. For a year, he spent nearly every night he had with his daughter at our house. We were used to simultaneously laughing and crying with him on a regular basis – we are tight to say the least.

His beautiful daughter forgot something at our house, and I went to drop it off one evening after work. As we were standing in the driveway, he said something about my birthday. Potentially, he was wishing me a happy, early birthday or asking me what I was doing on my day. Regardless, I will never forget that conversation. After a few minutes of chitchat, I finally confessed how much I was struggling. He said to me very straight-faced, "Why? It's just a number." I remember feeling silly about it, because in fact, it was just a number. But as I talked it out with him, I finally figured out what it was.

In my own terms, I had done a lot in my 20s. I had traveled to different parts of the world, had amazing adventures, started wonderful projects at work that were making a difference in communities, and I felt like people looked at me, including my friends, family, volunteers at my company and even peers and thought: She is living an extraordinary life. When I turned 30, I thought that people would want me to up the ante, or that they would expect a 30 year old to do those kind of wondrous things, automatically. Turning 30 meant that there was an expectation to do more and be more. Looking back, I know I really felt those things, but now, I love the experience of aging and turning the clock a year forward. I am so much more of me today than I ever was at 30 and I can't wait to hit another milestone, especially with how well my anti-wrinkle cream works.

When I think about bugs and birthdays, I know this list is not all encompassing, but it is important to identify the things that make me feel confident. This is the short list of some of the things that do not make me sweat, want to run and hide, or curl up in a ball. It feels good to create a list of things I do well, but this book is not about that – at all. This is a book about gaining confidence and I wanted to do that by owning what scares me so I can increase my confidence. So, here we go!

**I am afraid of failure.** There, I said it. Like most everyone else I know and love, I am terrified of a major work failure. It is interesting that I am not afraid of making mistakes, but a total failure makes me insanely nervous. I don't want to disappoint anyone and I don't want to live with the memory of a big let down. When I fail at something I can't let it go – for a long time. As much as I love opening my new business, I am so afraid to fail. I am afraid to let people down, but that is not the biggest part of this fear. I don't want people to think I can't accomplish what I want set out to do. I don't want to disappoint them or myself.

I am afraid that if I fail, people will think, "Oh, she failed at starting a new business; be careful of her." Also, I am afraid that they will only see my big failure and forget all of my accomplishments. I think that failures are a lot like a bad evaluation. My brain's recorder for taping failures rarely fails. I don't like false compliments either, so I always take them with a grain of salt. Like most people who are trying to be humble, I take the hard stuff really hard and the compliments as if they are not really directed at me.

**I am afraid to open up to people too much.** Gosh, this is so much harder than I thought. I am afraid of getting hurt so I avoid being vulnerable at all cost, until I really know someone. The problem is that it takes a long time to cultivate a great friendship, especially with busy women who have children, a job and a full life. I am afraid of over sharing, of being too open or too exposed. Often, I will say, "I'm like a European. It takes a long time to get to know me, but once you are in, I am loyal for life." If I am being honest, I am really afraid of the cultivating process. More than that, I hate idle chit-chat. It bores me, and even more, it exhausts me. I have been using that as an excuse to stay close to my really close friends.

"Great friendships are the key to the human experience. I am going to open up this year and be a lot more vulnerable."

Great friendships are key to the human experience. I am going to open up this year and be a lot more vulnerable.

**I am afraid of asking people for business.** My sales coach has pushed me to cold call, to hunt for business, and ask for referrals so I can continue to grow my facilitation and curriculum writing business. I can "farm" which is to say that if I have a client, I can ask for more business, propose great ideas and feel confident about all of it; but to "hunt" for new business makes me completely unnerved.

**I am afraid of a big section of people – highly confident people.** How ironic, I know. I am afraid of talking to really confident people the first time I meet them. For instance, I am considering a second business this year and when I met a leasing agent at a new retail space for a second business I am exploring; I felt nervous. This man was very handsome and extremely confident. When I decided to look at other spaces outside of his jurisdiction; he introduced me to his brother. This older brother is nice, but not nearly as cool and confident. When I met him; I wasn't nervous at all. Pretty people seem more confident and cool - these people intimidate me a bit, too. I will own that this may seem irrational, but I am trying to be as transparent, as possible.

**I am afraid of people saying no to me.** I am a strong woman, but I can't stand someone telling me no. This is not like a little kid who can't have a cookie before dinner, but it is about rejection. This fear ranges from when I want to make dinner or social plans and someone declines all the way to not getting business from a client. I hate the small and big rejections of the world. I am certain I am not alone, but it makes me think about how many times I have opted out of something because I avoid the "no."

My husband and I are very social people, and the other day, I texted five couples to see if they wanted to watch our college team play football. Every person said no, and I hated it. It was last minute, but I still hated hearing all of the reasons why people could not make it. I would never expect anyone to cancel a kid's soccer game or not attend a baby shower, but when I thought the odds were in my favor, I hated the rejection even more.

As you can imagine, this goes back to sales, too. My coach shared with me that I need to get really comfortable with people telling me no and moving on immediately. "A no is so much better than being left in limbo," he reminds me. I know of a speaker whose coach told her to get at least 10 nos a day. What!?!? That is a lot of rejection in one day. She said she did everything from asking for free coffee at Starbucks to asking for new business that she had no hope of getting. The end result, was overcoming this fear by practicing and getting comfortable with the no. Although, it reminds me of some 80s talk show host that uncovered the work of aversion therapy and made the entire audience hold a snake. I don't like snakes or hearing no.

So here it is, my list of tangible and very perceptible fears. These fears are reliable and steadfast. They have no problem showing up in the most inopportune moment and they have no regard for social grace or timing. They are in a relentless chase to feast like mold, making their way into every dark crevasse of my mind. They spread like a diligent wildfire that has not been tamed. But, I am on a mission to stop their invasion and move toward an authentic existence. I have been facilitating this concept for so many years that I am in full agreement with my brain that I will not be making an Olympic attempt to be superhuman. I have no desire to get rid of realistic or safety-driven fears, but rather to be mindful of my space and the way I project myself to the world.

So, I am checking off the first item on my list and uncovering the fears that get in the way of my confidence. Exposing them all with the hope that drawing them out of hiding will start to heal those fears.

## Consider this:

- What are you not afraid of, first?

- What are the fears that get in the way of your confidence?

- What do you want to happen after exposing your fears? (For example, I wanted to own them so I could begin to heal them.)

- How will this knowledge impact your confidence?

# 1.6

## A RELENTLESS INVENTORY OF MYSELF

**THERE WAS ONE THING LEFT TO DO.** It was taking stake of who I really am. I hate to be put in a box, and I don't want to settle or be incapable of chance, so I am paranoid of people describing me or categorizing me. Yet, I enthusiastically and insistently encourage all of my clients, friends and even my family members to take assessments - not the ones on Buzzfeed, but the ones like Strengths Finder 2.0 or the DiSC profile - partly so I can understand them better, but more so because I want them to work with their team/boss/partners/clients and even siblings/parents in a more thoughtful and intentional way. Even more so, we all need help removing our full-sized blind spots.

What I know is that humans are a lot like old radios. People are either tuning us in or tuning us out. We are in control of it, though. When my messages come in loud and clear, I tend to attract like-minded people. When my messages come in fuzzy or vague, I attract, well, nothing. I am way more interested in people who have the same values, but also push me to think differently and constructively.

Also, I am curious why some people are the way they are. I am curious why my husband can walk through a stadium and scream something after a big win and why 200 people will automatically respond. I am curious why my sister-in-law, Rachel,I has this magical power to raise truly thoughtful kids. Kids can be sweet, but thoughtful is an entirely different level. I am curious why my sales coach can make people talk about their deepest fears, and how my 94 year old grandma always holds court no matter where we are or what we are doing. I am a bit envious of these gregarious people, but more fascinated by what they send out that screams confidence.

When I started to unpack my personality profiles, I realized I was doing something that was a gift for me and for the people who I work with. Even more, I started to get clear on how to handle conflict better, ask more clearly for what I need in a relationship, talk to my clients in a way that honors their style, not just mine, and gain clarity around my frequency. All of the assessments over the years have lead me to worry less about being put in a box and more about getting a deeper understanding of my style. So, here I am:

**My top five strengths from Strengths Finder 2.0:**

1. Self-assurance®
   "People exceptionally talented in the Self-Assurance theme feel confident in their ability to manage their own lives. They possess an inner compass that gives them confidence that their decisions are right."

   WHAT THIS MEANS FOR ME:

   I am really comfortable in my own skin – which is a bit different than authentic confidence. I don't need confirmation from someone else to do what I believe is right. I am settled in my own ideas and thoughts, but sometimes lack the confidence to execute.

2. Maximizer®
   "People exceptionally talented in the Maximizer theme focus on strengths as a way to stimulate personal and group excellence. They seek to transform something strong into something superb."

   WHAT THIS MEANS FOR ME:

   Ah yes. I have to take everything to the next level. This is different than being a perfectionist or strategist. This is about the mastery of something. It plays out in my work for my favorite clients. I am in the constant pursuit of something more innovative, more fascinating, or more experiential.

3. Adaptability®
   "People exceptionally talented in the Adaptability theme prefer to go with the flow. They tend to be "now" people who take things as they come and discover the future one day at a time."

   | WHAT THIS MEANS FOR ME: |
   | --- |
   | Even though I want to maximize everything in my work life, I crave spontaneity and adventure. I always have a vision, but. I need to breath and be able to go with the flow or adapt in the moment. |

4. Connectedness®
   "People exceptionally talented in the Connectedness theme have faith in the links among all things. They believe there are few coincidences and that almost every event has meaning."

   | WHAT THIS MEANS FOR ME: |
   | --- |
   | Ah, my idealistic side. I am so practical in so many ways thanks to my Grandma Jane, but I am a deep thinker and always looking for the lesson and the meaning of things. |

5. Ideation®
   "People exceptionally talented in the Ideation theme are fascinated by ideas. They are able to find connections between seemingly disparate phenomena."

   | WHAT THIS MEANS FOR ME: |
   | --- |
   | Simply stated, I am a big time dreamer and idea maker. Recently, I have become very conscious that dreamers need to be doers, too, but I see the big puzzle of life and love how it all connects. |

There are 34 strengths in *Strengths Finder 2.0*, and your initial assessment outlines your top five.

**My love language is:**

1. Quality time

| WHAT THIS MEANS FOR ME: |
|---|
| I can buy my own presents, I have been independent my entire life, and don't need anyone to tell me I am doing great work, although it's always nice to hear. But, if you want to love on me, I want your undivided attention, I want you to run errands with me, see a movie with me, or even travel with me. I want you and your time. |

Gary Chapman is the author of the book *The Five Love Languages*. There are five love language that include: Quality time, acts of service, receiving gifts, physical touch and words of affirmation.

**My conflict style modes, in order, are:**

1. Competing
2. Collaborating

The Thomas-Kilmann Conflict Mode Instrument is a predictor of your conflict style. There are five options with two scales. On one scale is your level of assertiveness, and on the other scale is your level of cooperativeness. The five styles are competing, collaborating, compromising, avoiding and accommodating.

**Thomas Kilmann Conflict Mode Instrument**

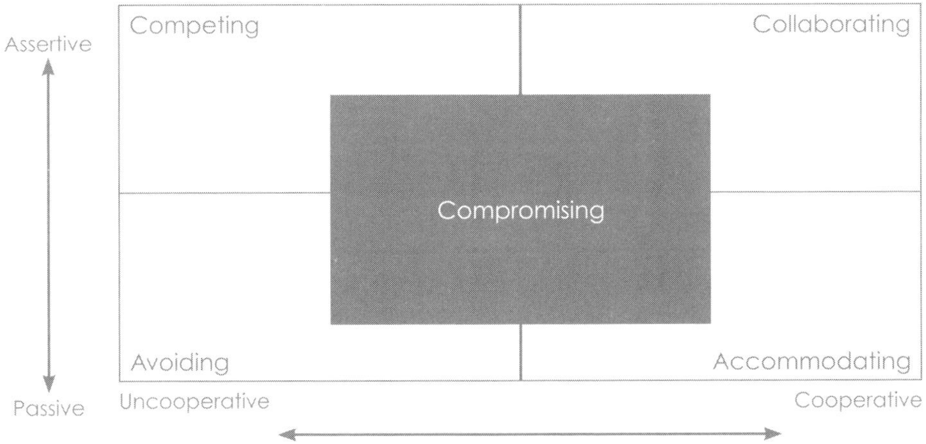

| WHAT THIS MEANS FOR ME: |
|---|
| There is no doubt of my assertiveness, and the list of people in my life who are willing to tell the tales is long; but I find that my style changes depending on who is in the room. If my mom is around, I find that I can be assertive on her behalf, but collaborative when she needs help at the holidays. When my dad is in the room, I can match his assertiveness. When I am traveling on my own, I am compromising because I hate the way adults treat people in the service industry. In some way, I am trying to balance out all of the bad people who think they run the world with their bad attitudes. I am keenly aware of other people's styles and I have become great at balancing what is needed through tough conversations. |

My DiSC profile:

1. I am a high D followed by being a high C
2. I am not an S, at all.

| | |
|---|---|
| D | Dreamers, drivers and change agents |
| i | Social, relationship-focused and optimistic |
| S | Analytical, steady, prefers not to change |
| C | In charge of process, organized and precise |

The DiSC profile outlines four main personality profiles. D stands for dominant, i stands for inspiring or influence, S stands for supportive/ steadiness and C stands for cautious/conscientiousness.

| WHAT THIS MEANS FOR ME: |
|---|
| My dad jokes, "Why do you take these assessments, I can tell you who you are – you are MY daughter." It's true. So much has changed since I was little, yet so much has stayed the same. I am quietly ambitious and a visionary (high on the D profile), Introverted (low on the i profile), wildly organized (high on the C scale), and have absolutely no desire to ever keep anything steady in my life (low on the S scale). |

On an even more personal level, I know I am a giver rather than a taker, I try to be a servant leader over ruling for my own advantage. I am a not a bystander, rather, I jump into situations when people are in trouble, even if it's none of my business. Just yesterday, I saw a two year old trying to jump out of a cart at Costco, and I told him to wait – at least until his mom saw his attempt at freedom. I am an animal lover and an ally to the LGBT + community. I am socially liberal and financially conservative. I love Target over Wal-Mart and I am certain that has something to do with my personality profile. I am a minimalist unless it's Christmas, but despise Halloween. I value buying the right thing, even if it costs more, as opposed to having a lot of stuff. I fully believe in Karma so I work to put good in the world, and I also believe in the Law of Attraction – which is understanding that like attracts like so I must be aware of my own thoughts so I can attract the right things in this world.

I crave structure and order, and my closet and car are always organized. When my house is a mess, I can't work. I am a list maker and love crossing things off – even writing things down that are done just so they can be marked. My calendar is color coded by client, and I even code personal events like parties and weddings. I require patience from anyone who travels or works with me. I hate perfection, but I demand excellence. I am shy over gregarious, and I am an excellent listener to other people's stories, and, I am the one that laughs at all the jokes, but never the joke teller. You need one of each in a relationship, I am convinced.

"I am shy over gregarious, and I am an excellent listener to other people's stories. I think this may be why it has taken me so long to write a book about my own journey."

I am a visual learner and could never remember a thing that my history professor droned on about in class. After being a visual learner, I am a full on kinesthetic learner. I need to try and fail, and that means I have to get my hands dirty. I believe in second chances, but not thirds. I value straight talk over reading between the lines. I never guess right there. I root for the underdog, unless they're playing my team. I always order the cheapest food on the menu if someone else is paying. I used to be afraid of eating a "real meal" in front of other women, but now I don't care. I don't need to eat a measly little salad to impress you.

I am a decent driver, but more importantly an awesome traveler who has mastered roving through all sorts of time zones. I am crazy patient until I am with someone who is impatient. For some reason, that makes me lose all of my patience. I am humble, but working on not being afraid of sharing my accomplishments with pride. I love getting dressed up about two times a year. Other than that, put me in jeans and a tee!

What I found, after I had gotten over my fear of being put in a box is that things become clear. I was no longer adapting to each new person – often confusing them when they finally saw the real me. Instead, my own confidence started to solidify and it felt crazy amazing. I also began to own that I am just fine being complex and layered. It's what makes me interesting. All of these little details that would normally ebb and flow based on who was in the room, started to be less of a distraction in my head because I let go of who I was supposed to be, and got more consumed by being interested in them - with all their fascinating, interesting, and complex layers.

## Consider this:

Whether or not you take these assessments, you have a general sense of your style, so don't worry about taking every online evaluation immediately. Rather, reflect on what you know to be true today.

- What are your strengths?
- What is your conflict style?
- What is your DiSC or personality profile?
- What else makes up who you are?
- How will this knowledge impact your confidence?

# Section Two:
# What I Learned Along the Way

what i learned along the way

# 2.1

## FIRST, PINTEREST HAS LED ME ASTRAY

Learning to Edit My Thoughts

**I AM HOOKED ON INSPIRATION**. I am a TED Talk watcher, a returning-home-from-the-service video junkie, and I can scroll through Pinterest for hours. Cats are cute, but I have a penchant for dogs, of course, and I love little kids who giggle hysterically. My new favorite viral video is the dad and baby saying "Wassup." I have collected hundreds of quotes online to use in my writing and in my keynote speeches. Some of my favorites right now are:

- "Worry is a misuse of your imagination."
- "If there are no ups and downs in your life, you are dead."
- "The unexpected is usually what brings the unbelievable."
- "I am currently under construction. Thanks for your patience."
- "Hustle hard girl."
- "Go the extra mile, it's never crowded."

My dilemma is that each time I find a great quote, I can undoubtedly and unquestionably find a quote that speaks as strongly and equally in the opposite direction.

Recently, I had to handle some really tough conversations with a few family members, and I found: *Be brave enough to start a conversation that matters.* Then, I scrolled down the long line and found one that said: *"Above anything, drink wine, first."* So, maybe I am supposed to drink wine before having a brave conversation? I really don't know.

*"Great things never came from comfort zones."* Yes. I love it. It's so true to me. Then, right next to the post called *15 Inspirational Quotes to Get You Through the Week is a quote that says: Master the art of observing.* Again, what am I supposed to do, wake up and go skydiving or watch the game from the sidelines?

"*'Great things never came from comfort zones.'*
Yes. I love it. It's so true to me."

Lately, I feel like there is some physics law that I am unaware of when it comes to getting a mastery of how to handle myself in situations that require my confidence. This is especially true when two things seem to be equally true and equally confusing. On top of it, I have been struggling with too much going on in my brain. I feel like I am over thinking – always trying and struggling to be in balance. Some days, I can wake up with total clarity and a structured to do list while other days, I can wake up and feel completely overwhelmed. So, instead of trying to have it all or be forced into balance, I am trying to surge and retreat on a few things.

Right now, I need to surge in the area of my health. I have put on pounds that I don't need, and I have been avoiding a few health screens and an outpatient procedure. My dad had cancer at 40 years old, and I too need to get my body checked regularly because of this health history. I find that going to the doctor is no big deal, but the embarrassment of extra weight is stopping me from getting real about what the cause is. The cancer screen and the increase of unexpected weight need to be my focus. On top of it, I need to get back to consistent exercise. Last summer I was hit with a frozen shoulder and shingles, but my excuses are out, and I have retreated for too long – it's time to surge and get into healthy habits again. Plus, I love yoga. Last Sunday, I went to a morning class with my two neighbors and felt incredible afterward. It's time to surge in the area of taking care of my body, again. I am sure I will find quotes online to support this!

I am also in the practice of retreating right now which can be equally as difficult if not harder. As a recovering people pleaser, I still struggle with loose ends to arguments. The kind where you can't make resolution happen, and you feel like you are not being heard or validated, or can't hear or validate either.

This fall, I had an unbearable conversation with a family member that lead to even more loose ends. This person in my life said terribly hurtful things that I just can't move past, right now. My natural tendency is to keep at it, to keep talking through things and to find common ground, but for some reason, this time it feels really different. Instead of doing what I normally do, I am letting go for a while. It has been heartbreaking and I have been up at night with anxiety thinking about my choice for weeks on end, but I am finally at a place of peace. I am not worried if I will be okay, but instead I am comfortable with the fact that sometimes everything can't be tied up in a few conversations. So, even though it's painful, there is peace right next to it. More than that, there are years of experience that remind me that I have other people on my team, and that I am not alone in going through times of disconnect and heartache.

So, instead of trying to figure out my life through a list of cute quotes that are masterfully designed, I have decided to be in the practice of being a critical thinker. I am going to give weight to the things that are most important right now, and let go of all of the mess in my brain that is doing a crazy game of tug-of-war. My confidence comes from being thoughtful and choosy, not perfect and balanced. So, I will surge and retreat, solve or let go, and start all over. I am working on authentic confidence – not movie star confidence with perfect hair and make-up, no blemishes, have-a-stylist confidence. I am working on clearing the chatter and occasional demons in my head kind of confidence.

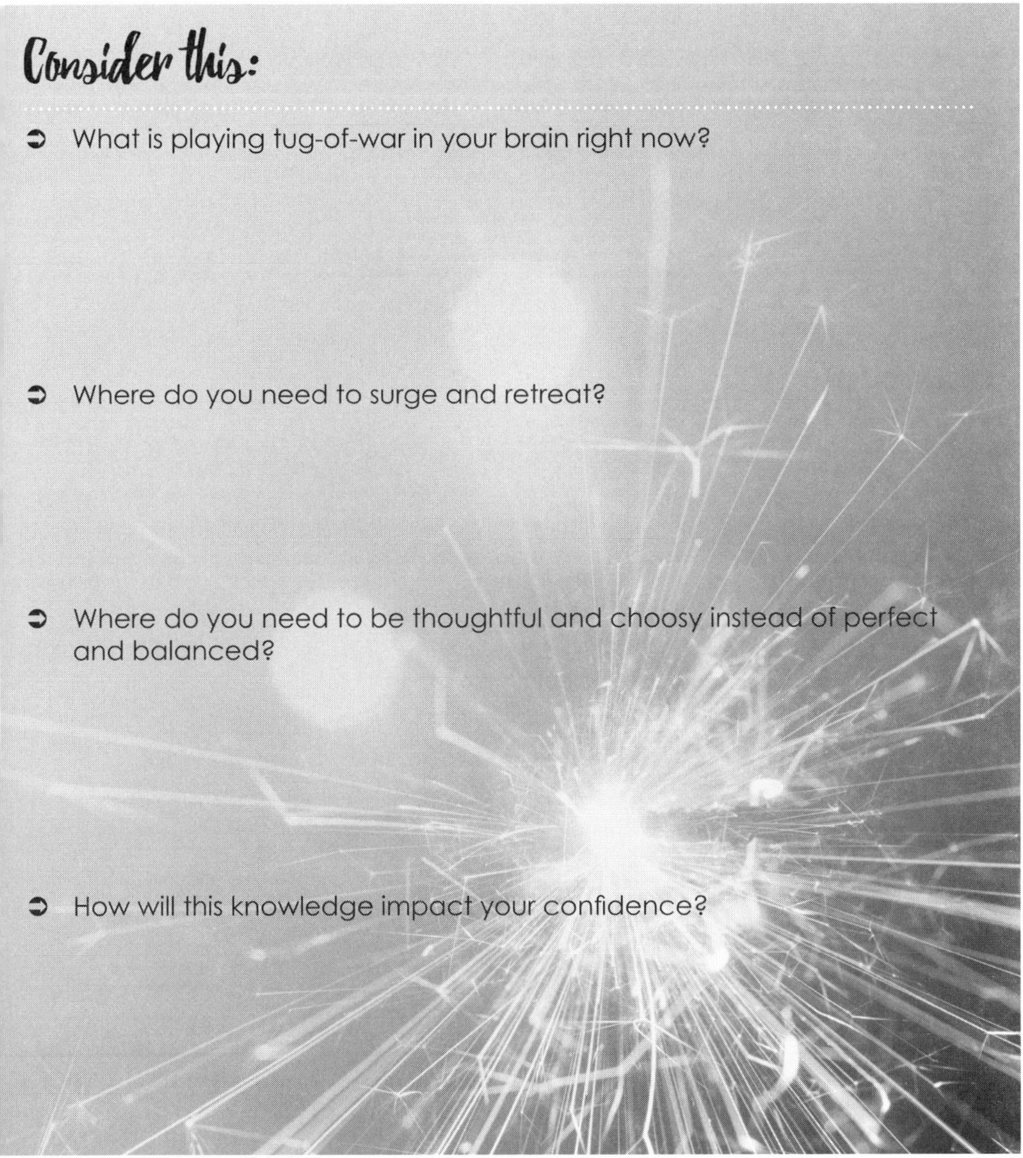

## Consider this:

- What is playing tug-of-war in your brain right now?

- Where do you need to surge and retreat?

- Where do you need to be thoughtful and choosy instead of perfect and balanced?

- How will this knowledge impact your confidence?

# 2.2

## THE LIFE OF A PANK

**THERE IS A STRONG SIDE OF ME THAT WANTS TO PURSUE MY PURPOSE, AND TO GET REALLY CLEAR ABOUT WHO I AM.** At the beginning of each of my keynotes, I share my life experiences through an explorative activity called: If you really knew me, you would know... I made this list two years ago, and each time I share it, I become increasingly comfortable in my own skin. Why? This list is a reminder of what I want to share with the outside world. I am really good at being a chameleon and adapting myself to the people around me. It's an immature way of trying to be cool. I am so over trying to be someone I am not, and I am much more interested in sharing my truths than trying to fit into yours. So, this list is a daily reminder of my values, my pursuits and my own passions, and it reminds me to get really clear about my own message and what puts me in charge of my own life.

For instance, if you really knew me, you would know that I am a voracious reader. I have hundreds of books in my house that are all about self-help, leadership development, marketing strategies for small business, and even books on creativity. I am hungry, thirsty and desperate for new knowledge. I am a deep thinker, a heavy processor, and love being in the practice of gaining a new awareness. I am not afraid to share that I am a leadership nerd. Well, I was, but I am in the practice of being confident. So, I will state it again. I am a leadership nerd.

If you really knew me, you would know that I crave travel. Some people crave brownies or a great glass of wine. I crave, with the same intensity, the sky. I have been traveling for work for 12 years, and it does not get old (unless it's winter in the Midwest and I can't find my car in the parking lot – that gets old!). I can still sit on a plane and be completely mesmerized at how small the trees are at 10,000 feet. I can get on a Subway or a Metro and feel total pleasure when I have figured out a new way of getting someplace old. On top of it, I love getting lost. It's so foreign to most people, but getting lost gets me some place I have never been. It's really the only time I believe in serendipity.

If you really knew me, you would know that I am an animal lover. My Yorkie is the love of my life. I am highly allergic to him, which is tragic and so ironic considering how much I love creatures. My husband says when he dies; he is coming back as my dog. There it is.

But, I lie awake in the middle of the winter worrying about animals out in the cold. I have to force myself to sleep so as not to be consumed by what potential abuse could be happening to a cat, a dog, a horse or some other domesticated animal.  After three allergy medicines, and a reminder that my little bub will only live for a few short more years, I am grateful for the peace I have when I am around something that is so gentle and would give anything to be near me. When we talk about nurture versus nature, I am sure that I saw my Grandmother Eva nurture every one of her horses and dogs, and it was a good example to see the love she shares with these beautiful creatures.

If you really knew me, you would know that at 16 years old, I decided that I never wanted kids. Although I have never shared this story out loud, I distinctly remember seeing a woman struggle with her toddler in a gigantic stroller, when I was younger. What I felt in that moment was so distinct. I felt like I had the choice between being all in and focused on a family, or having the freedom to serve in other ways. I remember feeling like having kids would be too much for me, and all these years later it is still true. I am so glad I honored that part of my being because it would have been easy to follow along with everyone else, but I am so glad I didn't. I had two people sternly say to me, "You will never know what it is like to be a parent." That is so true, but you will never know what it feels like not to be a parent. I am terrified of being alone in the end, I am prematurely sad that I will sit at dozens of weddings and feel like I will never be the mother of the bride, and I know I will never have the joy of having grandchildren. But I am proud of making my own choice. That makes me feel confident, even when people challenge me on my decision.

In so many ways, this has worked for me. I have traveled the world, but more importantly it has given me the freedom to help friends recover from divorce, which takes a full year of devotion, support and late night calls. In addition, it has recently given me the freedom to love on my 94 year old Grandma who just moved a mile away from me. Most importantly, it has given me the opportunity to be a certified PANK. This little society of PANKs is for Professional Aunts with No Kids. I feel crazy confident when I am being an aunt to my seven nieces and nephews.

"This little society of PANKs is for Professional Aunts with No Kids. I feel crazy confident when I am being an aunt to my seven nieces and nephews."

Two summers ago, I did something with the two oldest kids. I surprised them in Chicago for a concert. I took video of these two red heads as they were walking into the hotel – not knowing that I was in town. The seventeen year old picked me up, spun me around and in the deepest bass voice said, "No freakin' way!" It was the beginning of another adventure, with the sole focus of giving them my undivided time and energy.

Over 36 hours in Chicago, we ate German food, visited the coolest spot in town - the Eataly, picked up famous Chicago popcorn, visited a place that has an ATM cupcake dispenser, and then ate Girordano's pizza. You can clearly see the food theme that induced sleepiness from time to time. Finally, we went to see one of the best concerts of the summer: *Imagine Dragons*. There we were sitting in the front row watching this band rock. I could cry thinking about how much I love them and how much they mean to me, and then in the next breath I can think about how one of them will say something sassy and I will think, "Ah yes, they are still teenagers."

My life legacy is to be the world's best aunt, and I have made a pledge to give them my time and not just my money or a great birthday or Christmas gift. I want them to have access to me and set an example. My father has whispered, "You will be taken care of and loved, and in return don't pay it back to us, pay it forward to others."

Three summers ago, we did a trip to Colorado that I designated: Aunt Erin's Amazing Race. We did eleven activities in three, glorious days, and these beautiful red heads begged to go to bed each night. My favorite part was when Kyle said to me things like, "Can I tell you something you won't tell my mom." With a thoughtful smile, I always said yes. It meant that I had built enough love and trust over the years to be privy to the important stuff like the fact Kyle likes girls that have blonde hair but dark eyebrows. I got to know that Kaleigh is full of spunk and drama and that she craves understanding of the world, and she is beyond curious. She is a deep thinker and a non-stop processor.

I told these two that if I was going to be the worlds' best aunt, I needed them to take care of me when I got old. With no children of my own, I need a plan. They joked as we rafted by these big Colorado homes that they would buy me one when I retired.

When I am teaching Kyle to drive a stick shift, or Kaleigh wants to teach me how to do a smoky eye, I feel gratitude. It's my sweet spot. I am the niece/ nephew whisperer in some ways. I feel at my very best when I am in that role.

Finally, if you really knew me, you would know that I cry at the drop of a hat, crave change, and I am really stubborn. On top of it, I believe in fiscal responsibility while being socially liberal. And, by the way, I am not a bystander. Ever.

What I have learned is that we are all looking for a purpose, but there is also a caution in picking a focus. I have to be mindful of the difference between my roles and my identity. Roles like being a business owner, speaker, author, wife, daughter, or aunt can fade or be taken away with any set of chances or actions, but my identify can't. My identify is wrapped up in my values, beliefs and actions – my non-negotiables. I am working hard not to get wrapped up in the titles assigned to me, or even the ones I create. I am trying to focus on creating my core so if I lose anything, I will not be lost.

It's like a mother who sends her kids to college and realizes that she is no longer a full time, hands-on mom; or an executive retiring and realizing that she is no longer in charge of the daily sales strategy. All of these roles change and fade, but I have come to realize that, while they give me purpose, they can't be the only things that define me.

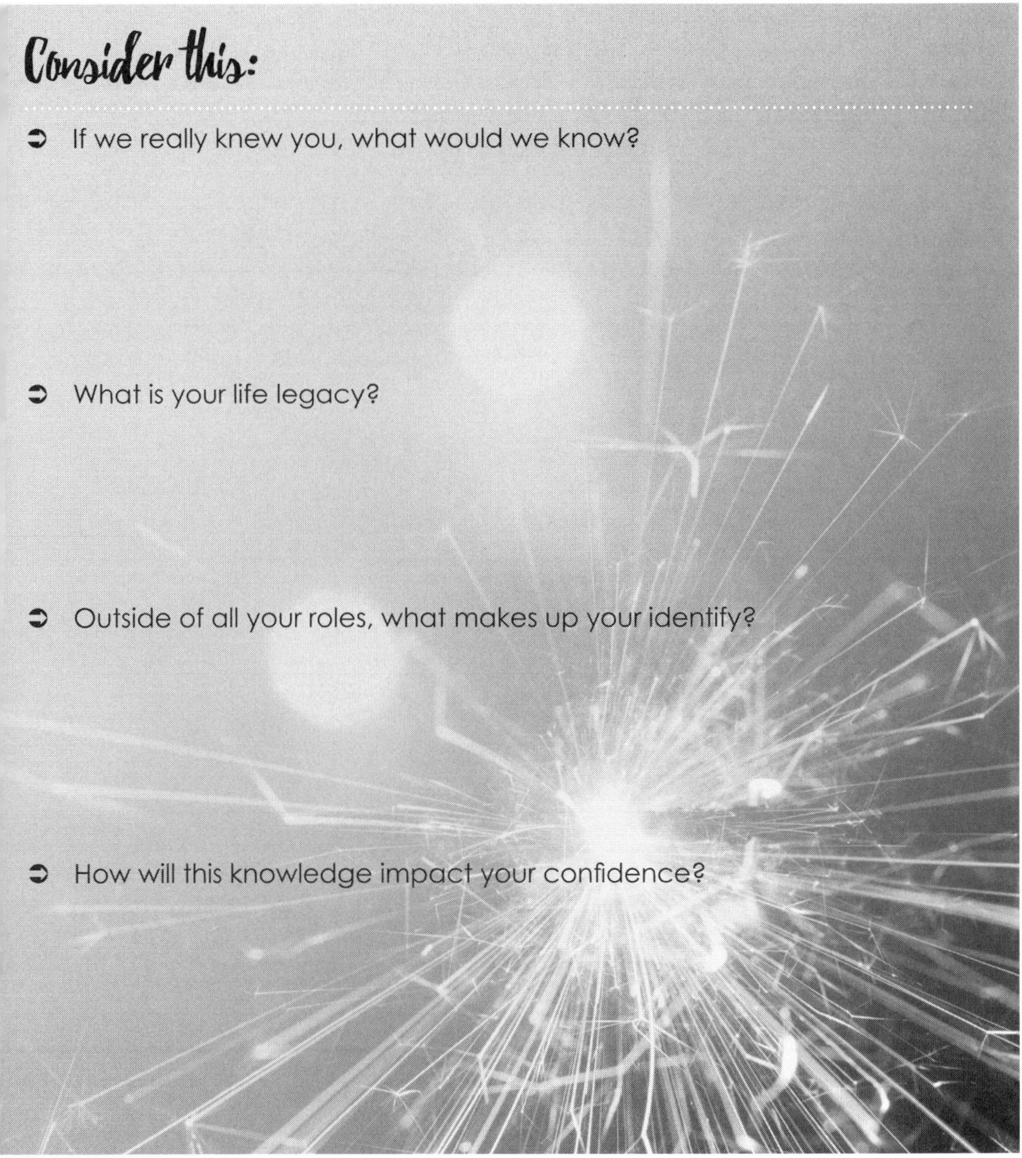

## Consider this:

➲ If we really knew you, what would we know?

➲ What is your life legacy?

➲ Outside of all your roles, what makes up your identify?

➲ How will this knowledge impact your confidence?

# what i learned along the way

# 2.3

## THE DOG'S WATER BOWL

**MY LITTLE YORKIE HAS BEEN IN MY LIFE FOR 15 YEARS, AND I NOTICED SOMETHING HORRIBLE RECENTLY.** Because he can't speak up, unless he wants my dinner, in which case he is a lunatic, he lives with a dirty water bowl, and, furthermore, he will never be able to complain about it. Sadly, it's probably why it doesn't go through the dishwasher as often as it should. He has never said, "Dude, how about a little attention to my bowl. You see that thing that looks like mold? I am here to tell you it probably is!"

Through this writing experience, I made a deeper observation about this. There are a lot of us, particularly women, who don't complain, don't speak up or don't ask for what we need. Two nights ago, I had dinner with my friend who was in town. Literally, as I was telling her how much I admire her fearlessness, she looked at me and said, "My sweet potato fries are burnt to a crisp. "Send them back!" I said. "Nope, it's fine." I was just telling her how much I admire her fearlessness, and yet she didn't send back her very expensive fries.

Right there, in that spot, I noticed something I have been seeing for years, but never could name before. It's this space of not wanting to take up space.

It's not just overcooked food, but it's a bad haircut, or even worse a bad hair color. (It is the only place I really invest any money, so it has to look good!) It is asking for the right salary, the right raise, or the right promotion. Furthermore, it is asking for the right supervisor, or better yet, the right leader. It's asking for the important project or the VIP client, or the travel that will allow me to do something magical while seeing some place magical. It is asking a partner to give me the right kind of love and attention, it is asking friends to wait for me, go ahead without me, or pay more attention to my struggle. It is asking the person in the movies to zip it up after the previews are over, and it's certainly asking the passenger sitting next to me to share that little, tiny elbow rest on the plane.

What I came to realize, is that it's in part about speaking up, but on a deeper level, it's the fear of someone else speaking up - about me.

I have been told I am high maintenance, a princess (only charming when my youngest brother calls me that on my birthday), am a have-to-have-it-my-way team member, and even picky. I know that other women have also been told they think they are better than everyone else, are too abrasive, or are not being humble enough when they ask for what they really want, or more importantly what they really need. Women are guilty of doing this to other women, too. In a thousand scenarios, I can hear, "Who does she think she is?" The equation is really simple:

A confident woman who asks for what she needs. = A woman who is full of herself.

It is disparaging and dejecting; yet there is nothing worse than needing something, and realizing that by speaking up or taking a stance I will be judged. Where did I learn that being quiet, being humble, or just being grateful for what I get is healthy? Hear me loud and clear, I am all about gratitude and humbleness, but there is a time in place in my life to be clear about my expectations.

**The new equation should read:**
A confident woman who asks for what she needs. = A woman who simply knows what she wants.

What ifs and wonders are all over my tally sheet. I can easily count the mistakes I've made and the things I regret – a decade of perms in my teenage years, not pushing hard enough to get on the volleyball team as a freshman, not breaking up with the wrong guy, not asking for a raise I wholeheartedly deserved when I worked at the YMCA, not listening to my voice when people were taking advantage of my kindness, and not using my voice when I needed to tell someone not to confuse my kindness for weakness. But one of the biggest ones is not using my voice as a woman to stand up for other women who simply need space and need to use their voice, too.

There is some force or power that prevents some women from being happy for other women, and I have named it the Too Much Syndrome. "She is too eager, too forceful, too powerful, too pretty, too ambitious, too full of herself to know that she should NOT be doing that." There is a lot of shaming when women rise to the top, and I feel like some women are taught to be the equalizers when someone is doing too well.

> "There is some force or power that prevents some women from being happy for other women, and I have named it Too Much Syndrome."

I can attribute some of my fault in this to jealousy, and some of it to the need for gossip in order to connect, but either way, I am instituting a personal resolution to mind the gap. I want to be conscious of how I support other women who are doing incredible things. Not because I have to, but because I must. Just like we are not running out of confidence in this world, we are not running out of greatness either. When amazing women do amazing things, we are all better for it. I must honor, lift up, coach, compliment and mentor because I firmly believe in the strength and competency of women.

Several years ago, I read a study that said women score higher in 15 out of

16 leadership competencies than men, so then where are all the women at the top? Is it lack of confidence? Is it lack of support? Is it women not sponsoring and supporting other women? You name it, but either way, I can have a small role in lifting up the work of other women in a meaningful way. I am skipping the, "Your dress is cute," and going for "Your work made me think in a way that I have never thought before." Plus, I am moving past the old notion that there can only be one spotlight in each room. Turn them all on. I am turning on every last spotlight for each woman bringing her A game. When women bring excellence, I am not going to walk away and tell someone else, or worse keep it to myself - so she won't get a big ego. I am going to walk up to her and tell her directly so she knows she has someone in her corner who thinks she is talented beyond measure.

Life is full of unexpected 'aha' moments, and today I am not short on any. I take back what I said about my Yorkie. I just realized as I was typing this chapter that I was all wrong about him. He really does ask for what he wants. As I pound away on this keyboard, he has made his way up to my typing fingers – pushing his little, wet nose into me, saying, "I need some love, attention and peanut butter. RIGHT NOW." So, there you have it, as I run downstairs for his afternoon peanut butter snack (let's own that he is high maintenance), I am taking stock in how he does speak up and asks for exactly what he wants – maybe I should take note.

# Consider this:

- Who are the people in your life that are not asking for what they need, and what can you do to better hear them?

- What do you need in your life? Who needs to know?

- How can you support women as their spotlight shines? (For instance, can you eliminate the Too Much speak?)

- How will this knowledge impact your confidence?

what i learned along the way

# 2.4

# THE FRENCH BOUNCER

Gaining New Experiences

**I CRIED WHEN MY DAD SAID GOODBYE TO ME AT THE CHICAGO AIRPORT.** I was the perfect combination of excited-out-of-my-mind and overwhelmed by the entire process of leaving my family for seven weeks to travel to Europe. This trip happened by no accident. I applied, and promptly thought I destroyed my chance during an interview in the fall of my junior year of high school. My only job during the interview was to identity all of the items on a dining room table in French – the fork, the knife, the plate, and the napkin. It was as if I never knew I was going to be asked to speak in French. I couldn't remember a single thing.

By some unknown force, or a really low standard of approval, I got a letter saying I was accepted. But, a quick reality check, and a hard conversation with my parents made me realize, we couldn't afford this little dream I had to see the world. I got a call weeks later asking if I was going or not, and then suddenly my great aunt passed. She left my grandmother money – almost the exact amount of the trip. Somehow, this money was being gifted to me, and it was remarkable. As I sit here writing, I don't think I could even process how lucky I was, in that moment.

It all happened so slow and yet so fast.

I remember getting on a massive plane after staying up most of the night saying goodbye to a high school boyfriend. He said he loved me for the first time, but I was headed to the most dazzling country in the world – France. I had visited there for a few days after my sophomore year in high school, but now I was headed there for an entire glorious summer. The simple rule was that once when we landed in Paris, we could not speak English for the next seven weeks. Oh, I had so much naivety (not to be confused with confidence, ever) that it didn't cross my mind that this would be hard – in any way. I remember napping on the plane window as we flew seven hours over to Europe and dreaming about the possibilities of this summer.

After struggling with my first family, I ended up with an eclectic, funny, sassy and fascinating French family. They lived in a walk-up apartment in the middle of downtown Brest – adjacent to every boulangerie and patisserie that would feed my need for bread, butter and chocolate. My French father drove a motorcycle to work year round, and my French mother smoked cigarettes in her fancy business suits. They gave me my own room with a tiny little view to the city, and I reveled in the fact that I had access to the world – at least my little part of it. I have no recollection of what they did for a living, but I remember thinking they had it right. They were dynamic and felt like home – although so different from my own. I fell in love with them and trusted them implicitly. They cared for me and helped me grow so much, but most importantly they bravely let me be me. They helped me practice my French, but when my French mother saw that I was tired, she would curtly tell her friends to stop talking to me. "She's exhausted – leave her alone," she would yell to them in her squeaky voice.

There were so many little adventures, including a few nights in Paris with some of my newest and closest friends, but the best part of all of it was when I tried every food that France had to offer. I started out as a size four and ended up as a size 10. That's right – I gained 20 pounds in seven weeks. On school days, I started out with fancy yogurt at home, and then stopped for a pain au chocolat on the way into class. I would eat a large sized dinner for lunch, a snack when I got home, then a full meal with cheese and dessert each and every night. My body was full of carbs and delicious delicacies, but I never worried about each pound – even when my new French knit dress began to stretch.

In between all of this eating, I spent some time learning the language – the real reason for the trip, I suppose. We would all spend our days at a school just outside of town, and from 9 until 2 pm, we would practice our grammar and our speaking skills. We were told on more than one occasion to stop saying 'merde' when we were upset by something. The innocence of the whole thing! During our lunch breaks, we would head outside to watch the high school sports teams practice while we sat in the sun, or listened to the Eagles on an old CD player. By the end of the summer, we knew every word to every song. I was happy and content in this little town on the seaboard. I was open, vulnerable, impressionable and learning a mile a minute. I was obliviously happy and drunk on the culture, and of course the people.

One of the most vivid memories happened about half way through my adventure to Europe. Somehow, all of the students convinced our families to take us to the Disco that came alive at midnight. If you knew me, you would know that I can rarely stay up past 10 pm, but there I stood, under-dressed, in jeans and a tee shirt, for a Disco - staring at a gigantic door not knowing how to get in to this unmarked place. My sweet and petite French father and I walked up to the door and spoke to the world's largest bouncer. In seconds, the cover charge was paid, and I was standing in a smoke filled room with hundreds of 18-25 year olds dancing to American music. It. Was. Perfection.

We danced and drank for hours until our French families came to pick us up in the middle of the summer night. My family teased me for days about a boy kissing me, and although I don't know how on Earth they found out about that, but I am sure my little grin gave it away.

When I look back, I think it was the happiest seven consecutive weeks of my entire life. I've had other joy that is indescribable after this fairy-tale trip, but I have never had consistent joy for such a sustained period. I was in love.

What I learned was that being out of my comfort zone is an amazing way to build confidence. Everything was new. It was the language, the French family, the city that seemed to wind in a thousand directions, new friendships to navigate, and even the incredible food. All of it made me miss home while simultaneously never wanting to return. The version of myself that was bred to be nice and compliant would have run from situations like the French bouncer, but instead, in this new freedom, I found that I was not scared of a whole lot. That French bouncer reminded me that when I am out of my comfort zone, I am growing. There is so much value in the stretch of life.

When put in uncomfortable situations, my natural tendency is to curl up, hide or even run. But, I don't want to live in a tiny little world full of creature comforts and sanity. I prefer the push and the grind. Comfy and cozy are good for a while, but I am in the pursuit of asking the universe for a challenge. When I am content, which I appreciate just as much as the push, I ask for something to help me grow. It is frightening, it hurts, it brings pain, but the end result is a new me.

"I prefer the push and the grind. Comfy and cozy are good for awhile, but I want to be in the pursuit of asking the universe for a challenge."

Then, decades passed, and I started to realize that it was becoming too simple to opt out of new and scary. Instead of practicing what I preach about resiliency, I started taking the easy way out. Simple. Unmarked, Nothing new. That had become my mantra. It is fraught with a subtle but heartbreaking realization that if you just stay steady, you can avoid all the potential pitfalls.

So, I have been more mindful of my rubber band analogy lately as I process my next steps into unchartered territory. I think that the rubber band is an incredible metaphor for how I want to live. While being mindful of the difference between stretching in this world (being realistic, collaborative, open to feedback, adaptive and expecting change), versus breaking in this world (folding up, storming off, blaming others, requiring control and having unrealistic expectations.) I am in the practice of growth – which means never going back to the same shape. Let me be clear and own that this is painful, it hurts, it brings heartache and fear, but, again, the end result is a new me.

I have decided I have a choice. Evolve or die. Well, die may be a little harsh, but evolve or stay the same? That seems even worse. I have no desire to stay exactly who I am today. So, with intent, I am going to put myself out there to see what door I knock on next.

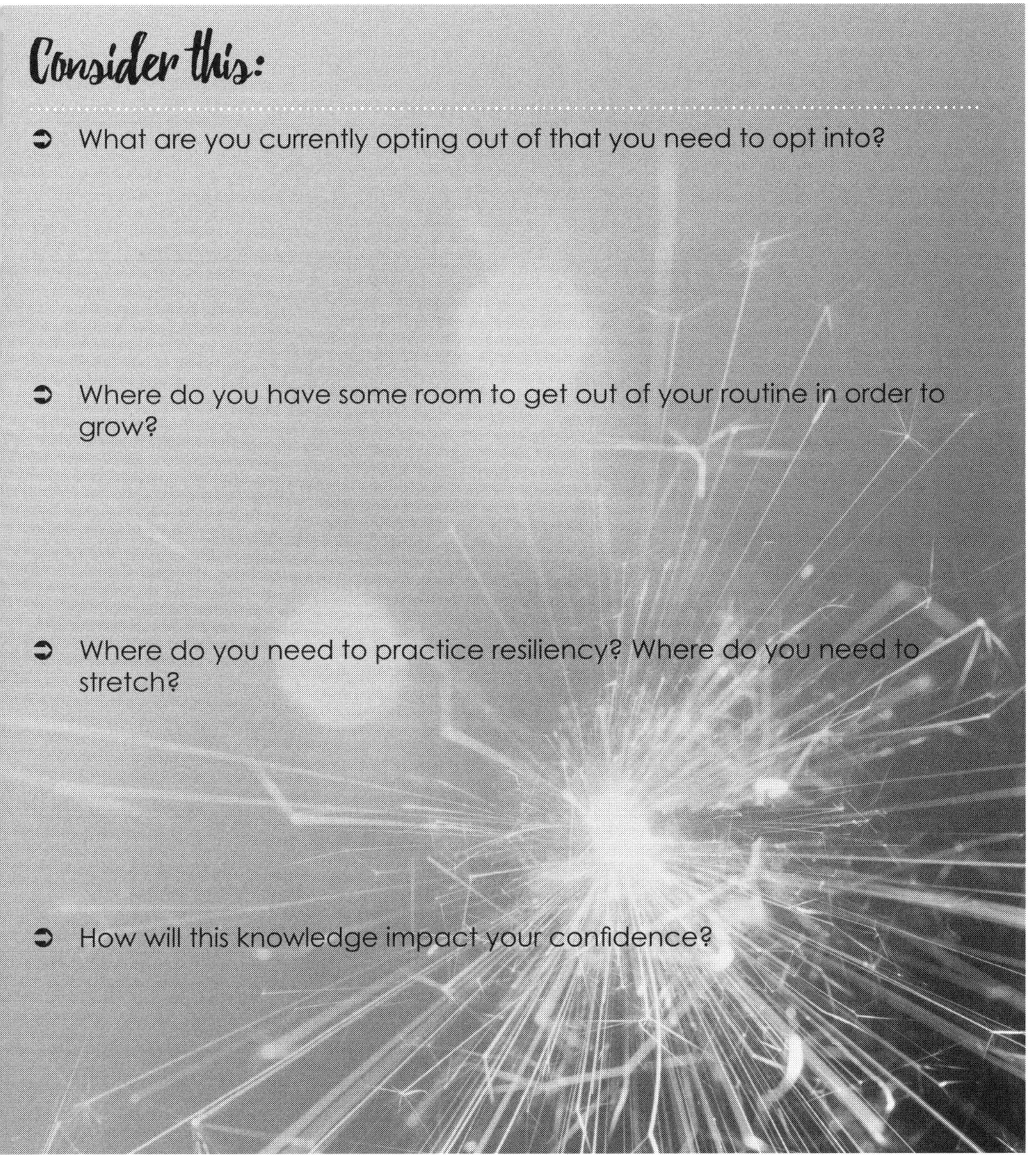

## Consider this:

- What are you currently opting out of that you need to opt into?

- Where do you have some room to get out of your routine in order to grow?

- Where do you need to practice resiliency? Where do you need to stretch?

- How will this knowledge impact your confidence?

# 2.5

## THE TUCSON TARGET

**MY MIDDLE SCHOOL FRIEND, LINDSAY AND I WERE ALWAYS THE TALLEST GIRLS IN SCHOOL,** and to this day, I still have height on my side, I have great wavy hair, and although I am not athletically inclined, I can water ski like no other -- thanks to one of my best friends, Mary Ann. I even started running 5Ks recently. My body is not a temple, but it is strong and resilient.

Despite all of this resiliency, I have cursed some of the genes I was given – no matter how much someone else would trade for them instantaneously – so much so that there are things that I do and don't do as a result of my self-consciousness. Wearing a comfortable swimsuit is one of them.

During two summers of my college career, I was working for a private camp on the Black River in the middle of Missouri . One time, I was brave enough to wear a bikini during a Sunday all-camp event, but I was self-conscious the entire day. I pulled and maneuvered uncomfortably for hours, and anytime there was a chance to have a towel wrapped around me, I took advantage of it. There was no reason, but for some reason, I could never wear a bikini again, until I got to the Target in Tucson.

This year, I was in Tucson for work, and all the hotels are beautiful resorts with big pools, water slides, swim up bars and even towel bars. It is hot in

Tucson in August. We are talking 100-degrees-at-8 pm-kind-of-hot. As I was driving to my hotel, I stopped by a Target to grab big bottles of water for my presentation the next day and a cord to charge my phone. I walked in and saw the line of clearance swimsuits, and for the first time in a million years, I picked up a bikini. Now, I am tall so there are times when a one piece is wildly uncomfortable because it stretches my torso into weird configurations and makes me feel like I have a permanent wedgie. However, it covers everything I want it to cover. For some reason, on this day, when I knew I would not run into anyone I knew, I picked up a two piece.

I have done a lot more important things in my life than buy a two piece. Let's be clear, this is a first world issue, but this little purchase gave me some power. I was not ashamed of my body, and more than that, I realized something. My lack of confidence in a swimsuit was lined up around what other people would think about my body, but rarely about what I thought.

There are times when I admire my friends perfect and petite bodies at our annual lake pilgrimage, but for the most part, no one gives a damn about what everyone else looks like. No one is whispering about who had doughnuts for dinner or beer for breakfast. There is no chatter around people's imperfections, yet my own head space had been wrapped around what everyone else thinks. So, I marched into the hotel, checked in, put on that suit, and went straight to the pool.

It was tough for about twenty minutes, and then with each minute or two, I started to care less and less. I read a magazine, got some sun and went back to my room. A tiny change in my brain started to happen. For the two days I was in Tucson, I started to notice every time I was conscious about my body's imperfections. Then, I would start with some clear self-talk around the value I am placing on my body. I wish my stomach was a little flatter and my arms were much tighter, but on the whole, I don't want my confidence to come from how cute my swimsuit is or how good I look in it. I want my value to come from how smart I am, how good I am at my job, how awesome of an aunt I am, and how kind I am to others. I must get out of my head.

Recently, a friend of mine shared her personal struggle with weight, and how much pressure there is to be a certain size. She shared how conscious she is in a room with colleagues after some unexpected extra pounds, and how this weight clouds her mind because it's all she can think about. In a matter of 24 hours, a new professional I was facilitating to shared the same struggle. "How can you be happy and confident when you're conscious of your body – all the time?" she asked. "I don't know, I am working on that myself." If it's not weight, it is always something else.

Knobby knees, crooked teeth from not wearing my retainer (sorry, Mom!) – even gray hair. I can make a long list of all the things I want to be different externally, but it's foolish and will do nothing but create a visual reminder of the things I already know. Plus, I never, ever want my nieces to hear me say things like, "It's time to start a big diet after the holidays." or "I have got to lose some weight before my next trip/event/wedding/speaking gig." I can get around sharing a vision of great health so I can live a long time for them, but I fear it is sending a message to soon that external perfection is what we are striving for as adult women.

It's true, I do feel best when I look my best, but I am not willing to put the pressure on myself to look perfect in order to get to get false confidence. Since I am an author and speaker, I get inspiration and stories around the clock. I started writing them on my mirror. Here is a list of things I am focusing on instead of fixating on what I don't like. I reminded myself not to be a Jill-of-all-trades, but to be exceptional at a few important items.

1. I am great at being a highly involved aunt.
2. I am a clever and thoughtful speaker on the topic of confidence for women.
3. I am wickedly organized, and equally adaptable.
4. I can take really tough topics and make them easy for people to understand.
5. I can keep kids engaged in games and activities for seven days straight thanks to my camping background. Even though I don't have kids, this comes in handy more than anyone would guess.
6. I am a phenomenal traveler, a leadership nerd and a woman on a mission to help other women find confidence.

And that's enough for me.

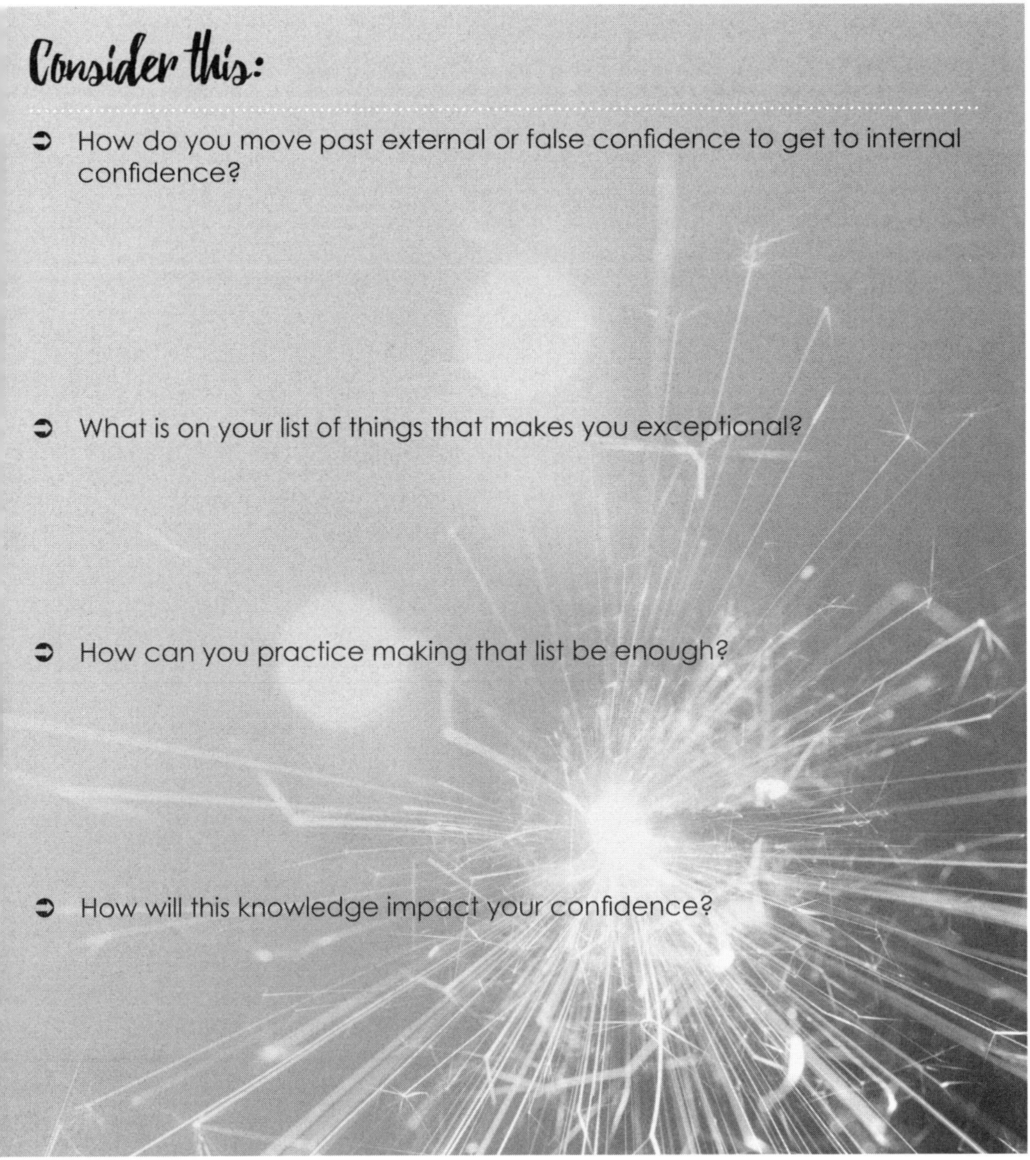

## Consider this:

- How do you move past external or false confidence to get to internal confidence?

- What is on your list of things that makes you exceptional?

- How can you practice making that list be enough?

- How will this knowledge impact your confidence?

# what i learned along the way

# 2.6

# CHRISTMAS LISTS AND BUSINESS LISTS

**WHEN I AM OVERWHELMED OR ACTING LIKE THE KID WHOSE HALLOWEEN CANDY WAS STOLEN,** I find that my confidence tanks. Being overwhelmed makes me feel like I am incompetent, and my natural tendency is to do nothing over doing something. This is everything from term papers in college to job applications that are 23 pages long. It is finding the starting point for a two year project with 33 new leadership courses and also writing a business plan for my new business idea. I am not a procrastinator, I never wait until the last minute, but I struggle with the start. Then, I got a fix.

For some reason, I have a relatively new, but very true fascination and occupation with the holidays. When I was little, like most kids, I loved getting Christmas presents, and I loved seeing my two sweet Grandmas who would drive up for the long weekend together from St. Louis. Even though we came from a modest family, my mom would make a Christmas brunch that we would dress for. (No xmas pj's for Patrick, Jack and me.) We would eat off china and had to wait to open up our gifts until everyone had coffee, fruit, and Christmas casserole.

After a torturing long brunch, we would open presents while eating the thousands of snacks they would bring for us. Better Cheddars, Chex Mix, and M&M's, and Milano cookies. I loved Christmas, but not like I love it now.

A few years ago something ignited and inspired me. Now, with even more desperation, I wish to get through September and October so that I can decorate my house for Christmas. Unwillingly, I fill my house with a few fall treasures like my coveted mercury glass pumpkins, but my heart belongs to St. Nick. My tree comes out the weekend (or two) before Thanksgiving, and it stands with all of it's silver ornaments and ribbons for six full weeks.

What I know to be true about Christmas is that it is easy. I have a master checklist of presents to purchase. I pick out one piece of fruit and have a theme of meals and hors d'oeuvres around that fruit. A few years ago it was pears. We had pears in our salad, pear sweet bread as a side dish, and chocolate dipped pears for dessert. And, I make plans with family friends to do a ring and run for a family with lots of great kids, but not a lot of money. (I cry like a baby every time when I see their faces in the windows after we deliver dozens of presents from Santa.)

But what I have found is that when something is fun, easy or I have done it a dozen times, it's not hard to accomplish. When something is daunting, hard or brand new – it scares me into indecision. So, I started a new practice. I started writing lists just like I do at the holidays. This is a little different than a to-do list. This is a get-your-head-wrapped-around-this-project list or a you-are-braver-than-you-think list. It's not just a checklist, it's a reality check on my capacity and capability. I am naturally drawn to change, creativity, newness, and a challenge, but even so, I can easily put off big projects because I can't or don't know how to see what I need to do.

So, a year ago, when I was contemplating writing a new book, now called *The Freshman Project* for my nieces and nephews about the college experience, I practiced this habit of creating an initial list that was short and sweet, but encompassed all the major obstacles I would have to overcome to take this idea from conception to a completed project.

I created a few assumptions about this project, first. It would be dedicated to my nieces and nephews, it would be about the freshman experience, it would be short articles on a multitude of topics, and the topics would be about the tough stuff parents didn't know or didn't want to talk about. Once I made up my mind about that, I created a you-are-braver-than-you-think list.

Here is what I wrote down:

- Create a list of topics. (We ended up with 25 topics.)
- Find experts in each area. (We ended up with about 20 experts in higher education.)
- Set up a contract with each author. (We found the publisher first and she had a contract that we updated.)
- Find a publisher. (I reached out to the people I knew who had written books and asked for their advice. By the way, this was not a huge publishing house in New York City. This was a small publisher with some great experience. )
- Find an editor. (We had four editors – and regretfully, there are still some mistakes.)
- Find a printing house. (Our publisher was great at that, too.)

It was still intimidating as hell, and there were plenty of times during the collaboration process that I thought I was in over my head, but this process let me create some bumpers, and this was the proof I needed to know that I could do these things. I will admit that it also helped that I had a few friends who had written books. I had the mindset that if they could do it, so could I. But more importantly, when I looked at this list, it was not overwhelming – at all.

I make these lists every time something scary and overwhelming comes up in my life. How will I hit my sales goal? My sales coach encouraged me to simply write down my goal number, list the products I offer, then determine how much I need to sell of each of these items to hit my goal.

- Write my sales goal.
- Write down my products.
- Run the numbers on each product and find out how much of each product I need to sell.
- Put it in a spread sheet, and make the calls.

Right now, I want to be healthy, so my list is:

- Eat protein twice a day. (This is really hard as a vegetarian.)
- Drink five bottles of water each day. (I am constantly peeing.)
- Take a probiotic to keep my body in check.
- Don't eat sugar and bread!

I am such a visual learner, so this is invaluable for me to see all the time. When I look at these lists two things happen. First, I realize how easy my goals really are, and then I see the real line between being a starter of an idea and my confidence around my capability. I am leaning into a new truth. There are very few things that are too hard to do. Let's take out anything in the medical field (kudos to you who are!) or anything to do with the mechanics of creating a building (thankfully my dad is an architect so I have that covered).

> "I am leaning into a new truth.
> There are very few things that are too hard to do."

However, after taking a few daring things off the list, like being an astronaut, I have realized my biggest ambitions are not that hard – they are just hard to start. So, my alignment is not how smart I am, but more so what I am willing to give energy to. I am removing the roadblock of that's-not-in-my-area-of-expertise to that's not in my area of study/interest/passion or must-do-to-breathe-and-be-happy list. My gut says there are a lot of roadblocks, but when I clearly and visually see my list, it moves things from impossible to inevitable.

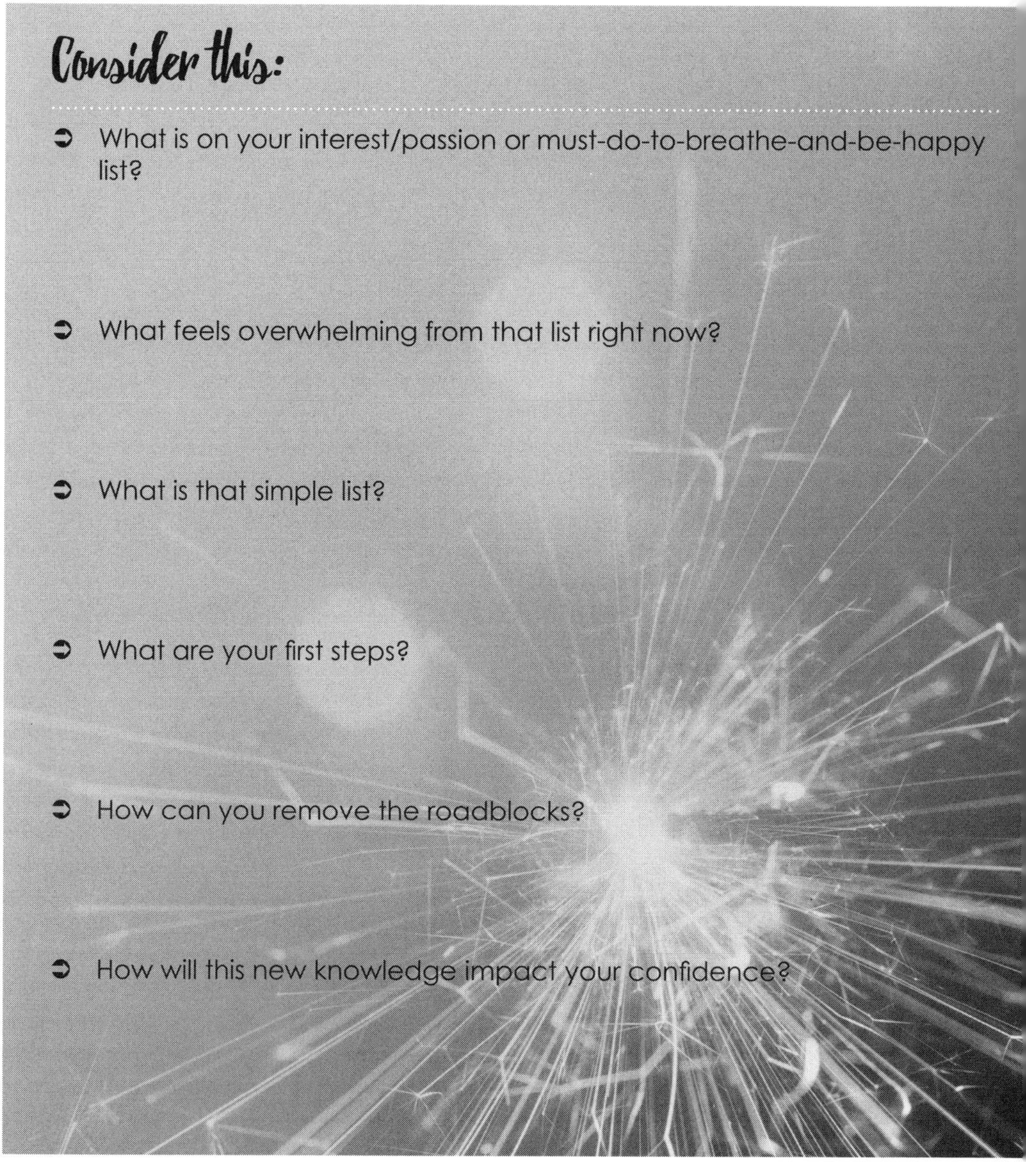

## Consider this:

- What is on your interest/passion or must-do-to-breathe-and-be-happy list?

- What feels overwhelming from that list right now?

- What is that simple list?

- What are your first steps?

- How can you remove the roadblocks?

- How will this new knowledge impact your confidence?

# 2.7

# ALBERT BRENNAMAN HAS IT FIGURED OUT

*Identifying My Confidence Mentor*

**FOR SOME REASON, I HAVE THE WORST TIME FINDING MY WAY AROUND A NEW CAMPUS WHEN I KEYNOTE.** Usually, I am given a PDF map that has been copied and scanned a dozen times, or I have a faculty member tell me to meet them at the Student Union. The problem is, I have no idea where that Student Union is, and more than that, I have no idea where to park when I finally find it. Then, I got a chance to speak at a small campus on a beautiful cliff that overlooks a massive, winding river. It is quaint to say the least, and on top of it, there is no way to get confused or lost. When I arrived, I started pulling all of my supplies out of my car. I had guides, speakers, a laptop, a thousand cords, and a suit bag of clothes to change into.

As I was standing on the sidewalk, I saw a young, athletic, college man coming from across the quad with his Beats in his ears. That guy did not even make eye contact with me, even though there was no one else around. He was trying so hard to be so cool – you could see it in his swagger, and in the way he got so close to me, but you could tell, in his mind, I was so far from him.

That night, as I was speaking, I shared the story about this guy trying to be detached, and I also shared that I think there is a huge difference between being confident and trying to be cool. Cool is me trying to be impressive, trying to prove that I have all my stuff together, even when I don't, and telling you about how amazing my life is, even when it's not. It is about being the hero of a story that doesn't even exist.

Confidence is when I am in that sweet spot of knowing what I know, knowing what I don't know, and knowing the difference, and it is about owning exactly who I am, even when it is unpopular or uncool. It is being really comfortable being the nerd when everyone else is trying to be the princess – or vice versa.

I have struggled and even vacillated for years between feeling cool and totally uncertain, so I started jotting down notes about when I felt something strong in any of these categories. I wanted to find the pattern of emotions attached to the sweet spot of authentic confidence.

| OVER CONFIDENCE/COOLNESS |
| --- |
| ♦ Feeling the need to impress everyone.<br>♦ Making sure everyone knows how much better you are than them.<br>♦ Pretending to be someone you are not.<br>♦ Being exhausted all the time from trying to be cool.<br>♦ Concentrating on yourself instead of connecting with others.<br>♦ **WORRYING ABOUT BEING LIKED.** |
| AUTHENTIC CONFIDENCE/SWEET SPOT |
| ♦ Being comfortable in your own skin.<br>♦ Knowing your values and actually putting them into action.<br>♦ Being silly if you are silly and being serious if you are serious. But always being mindful of others.<br>♦ Realizing who you are and who you are not, and not worrying about it.<br>♦ Going on despite what everyone else thinks.<br>♦ Showcasing your strengths even when they are different from everyone else.<br>♦ **WORRYING ABOUT MAKING A DIFFERENCE.** |
| UNDER CONFIDENCE/UNCERTAINTY |
| ♦ Being concerned about what everyone else thinks.<br>♦ Needing constant approval.<br>♦ Opting out of important life moments because of anxiety.<br>♦ Holding back the best part for fear of judgment.<br>♦ Rating yourself against everyone and always thinking you are less.<br>♦ **WORRYING ABOUT MAKING A MISTAKE.** |

My biggest take-a-way is that authentic confidence comes in the form of an overweight, shy accountant who relies on an inhaler during big moments. His name is Albert Brennaman. Even though he is this sweet fictional character from the movie *Hitch*, he is my inspiration for authentic confidence.

He asks a date doctor to land him a date with the women of his dreams, but instead of following all of Hitch's rules, he dances like a maniac, kisses the girl after chucking his inhaler, and makes a fool out of himself after losing her – the first time.

All along, he thought he had to impress her, and all along, he just had to be himself. Brilliant. Really hard to do in real life, but it's brilliant. He is the guy that gets the girl and gets married in the end. Not the perfect, masterfully put together date doctor, but instead, the big goofball ends up married He is the awkward one with a bad haircut, a boring job, and a bold soul.

It reminds me of a student I met in a small college town in Texas. I was there observing a new program I wrote, and at the end of our 60 minutes together, she boldly stood up and said, "Remember, we have a dance tomorrow night, and remember I am socially awkward and have no idea how to put myself together. I am your project. So, what time are we meeting to get me ready?" There she was, totally confident. She was part bold, part awkward, and part perfect.

I have realized, I crave real. I am attracted to people who have some of their stuff together, and can also share when they are a hot mess, and, I am equally terrified of people who only show me their pretty and perfect side. It makes me not trust them because I feel like they are holding back. Maybe it's because they don't want to scare anyone away. I am certainly cautious of people who will steal all of my emotional support, but I learned that I crave deep conversations with real humans who are having the full life experience. Not just the ones who have it together for this minute.

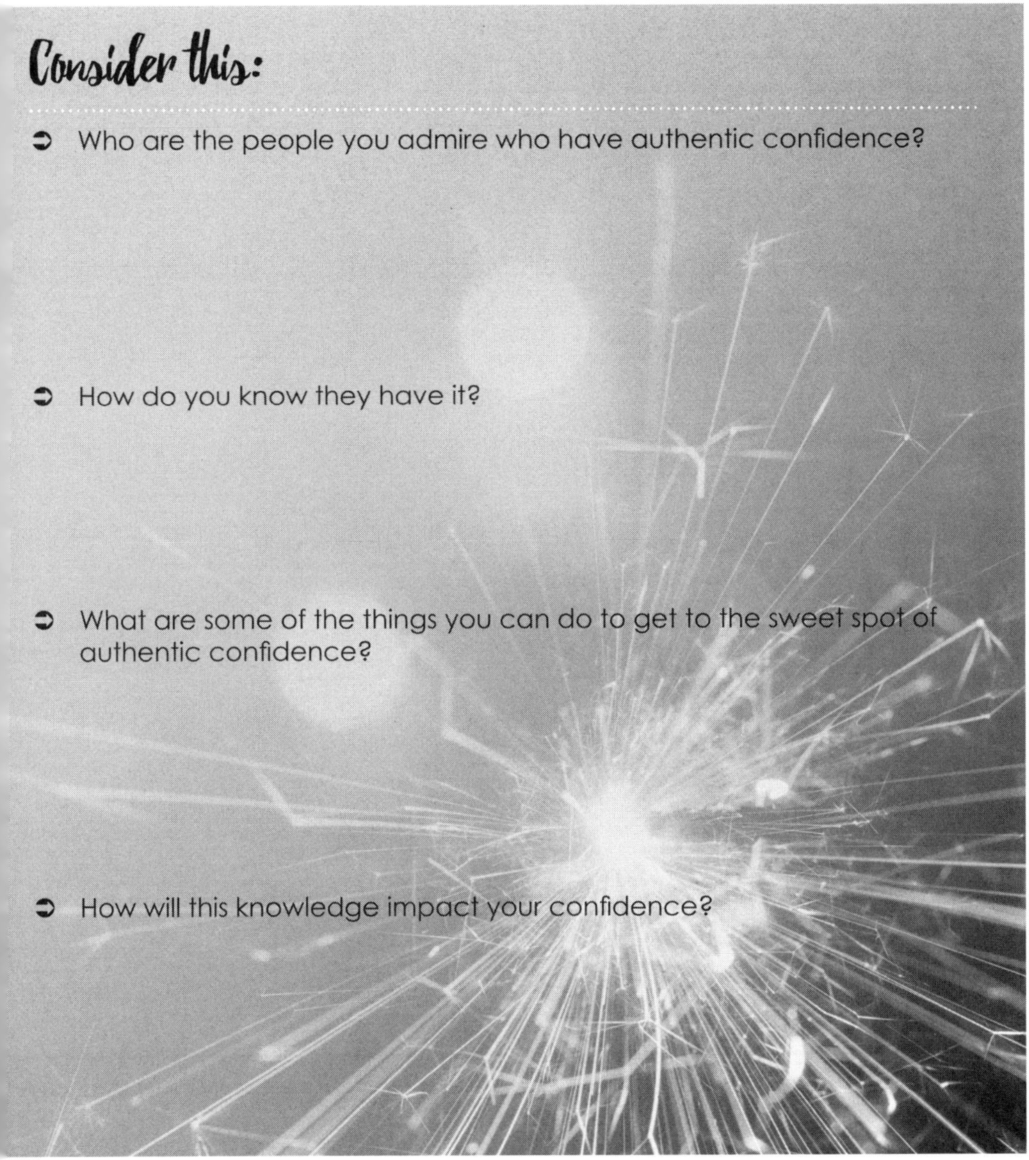

## Consider this:

- Who are the people you admire who have authentic confidence?

- How do you know they have it?

- What are some of the things you can do to get to the sweet spot of authentic confidence?

- How will this knowledge impact your confidence?

what i learned along the way

# 2.8

# THE SMALLEST CALIFORNIA AIRPORT AND THE LOUDEST HIGHWAY

**A FEW YEARS AGO, I WAS IN THE DESERT OF CALIFORNIA FOR AN EVENT FOR A TRADE ASSOCIATION.** I delivered a program and then got to sit by the pool with my friend Gabby – a perk of working in an industry where most everyone is a friend as well as a colleague. It is regular for me to travel a fair amount, and be in and out of conference hotels, airports and meeting rooms. The day after my event in the desert, I drove back to the small Ontario, CA. airport.

Most people know that I am a vegetarian, and at the time, I was fairly new to this practice. So, finding something to eat in a tiny airport with just a few gates was proving to be challenging. I strolled around for a bit and settled on a pizza place that served pre-made salads. As I jumped into the line with my salad, all of a sudden I realized in a very short period of time that the place was jumping. While there was no one in line just a few minutes earlier, there seemed to be dozens of people waiting to get pizza. As I stood waiting to pay, I noticed there were three people in front of me. The first one in line was a woman in her 40s, behind her was a man in his 60s and behind him and in front of me was a very tall gentleman in his 30s or 40s.

As we were all standing there, I heard a little noise. I am a nosy person, so I perked up and leaned in to hear what was going on. It was disturbing.

The first gentleman was yelling at the women in front of him. He was being rude and aggressive, and what I finally learned was that he was screeching, "This is America. We speak English in America!" What I later learned is that the woman at the counter, paying for her meal, was being spoken to in Spanish by another woman running the cash register, and naturally she responded back in her native language.

Now, this is one of the times in my life when I felt like there was not enough deodorant in the world to handle the sweat pouring out of my body. I was hot, I was mad, I was pissed off, and I was starting to debate exactly what I was going to do – or not do.

So, the woman quietly paid for her meal, the screaming man paid for his meal, the tall gentleman in front of me paid for his, and I followed. After grabbing my salad and drink, I boldly walked over to this man and did what I never thought I would do. I confronted him. I pulled out my pointy finger and like a teacher leaned over him as he sat with his food, and I said to him, "No one, and I mean no one talks to women that way, in my presence. Do you understand me?" Really? I was threatening him like a parent or a teacher, or even a mother. I didn't really think all of this through.

What happened next was a series of unexpected events. First, the man said, "If you don't move…now…right now, I will pour this soda all over you." I can't remember if I said anything next, but I do remember walking away within a few moments. Then, as I started walking toward my gate, I got another burst of boldness as I walked by the security screening area. I simply stopped an officer and told him everything that happened, and how I thought this guy was a threat to this woman. I will never forget how he listened so kindly and intently to me, and then said the only thing I could have ever dreamed, but never guessed. He leaned over and shared, "Don't worry, that guy won't be flying on any plane, today."

My whole body was a bunch of crazy nerves and wild energy. I kept thinking that either my body might explode into a million pieces or that I would break down and start bawling. People would assume that I was leaving a loved one, or going away to some far off land – never to return. But, I held it together, until I saw the sweet woman. This is the woman who was the first one in my line, the woman that was aggressively dismissed, and the woman who was now standing in the same bookstore as me. I looked at her and all my emotions let go. I cried like a baby, and at one point asked her if she could give me a hug.

As my tears stopped, I began to tell her the story of what happened and my follow up conversation with the security officer. I told her that she did not have to worry about leaving this small airport on a small plane and being stuck with this small minded man sitting anywhere near her. She was relieved and then told me her tale.

She said that she was bilingual and as an immigrant, she normally speaks English to stay in practice, but for some reason the woman running the cash register knew she was a Spanish speaker and started their transaction in Spanish. She told me to be respectful, she immediately responded in the same way. Then, she shared that she was surprised and shocked that I spoke up, but she was proud that her son saw the entire thing – including my conversation with the man. She shared that no one sticks up for her, and she and her son are often in these types of situations. I cried more, and realized that while she was safe for today, she was not always safe from these kinds of cruel circumstances.

Then, I got on my plane. I sat down for the first time, and let it all sink in. As I was in a really deep, exhaustive kind of thought, I heard the person sitting across the aisle start to speak to me. He said, "What the hell just happened back there?" It was the man who was standing in front of me in that line. The really tall one in his 30s or 40s. All of a sudden this story was all coming full circle, again. He leaned over to me after I shared the entire story and he said, "Man, I wish I would have stepped up and said something." Me too, buddy, me, too.

In this smallest California airport, in one of the largest states in the U.S., I had a huge 'aha' moment. My confidence comes from doing brave things, and my confidence is increased when I am not a bystander in this world. I realized that authentic confidence can come with a lot of emotions. I can spontaneously and easily feel confident and scared out of my mind – in the same moment. I can feel confident and sad, confident and bold, or confident and overwhelmed. It does not seem to be a singular emotion for me, and what I learned is that it feels good to do the right thing – even when it comes with a layer of other emotions.

Most recently, I was driving home from my home airport. I have a rule that when I land, I have to put my game face on. I am away from home a lot and owe it to my husband to be ready to engage in life – even when I am exhausted. So, I had my music blaring in my old Jeep Wrangler when I saw a fire on the highway.

"Universe, are you sure? I am tired, and I am trying to find some energy before I walk in the door." But I do remember asking the universe to give me something interesting and to be challenged a few years ago. My request must have not worn off, yet. Knowing that I hate regret more than anything, I pulled over the median and realized that a car was burning what seemed to be a million degrees of heat. There was a young man who stopped before me, too. And as he was standing at the median, I screamed over the highway's noise and said, "We have to go. Are you ready?" He looked over at me and said, "Yes, but lady, you are wearing heels." I laughed at the universe, again.

Somehow, we both made this instant, quick decision to jump the median, but I couldn't get my hiny over the median barricades. He kept asking me if I wanted help, and finally I obliged. Out of nowhere, I grabbed his hand and screamed, "This is like frogger. At some point, we are going to have to run across these lanes." As I started to make a go, his hand pulled me back. I had totally missed a car barreling in between lanes, and on top of it he heard something that I didn't. There was another woman closer to the car on fire who shouted, "They are all out! They are all out of the car. Can you hear me? They are all out!"

Within seconds or minutes, and I don't know which, we heard the fire trucks. We stared at the whole scene for several minutes and then realized we were in danger, too. We should not be in the middle of the highway! So, my new friend managed to gracefully get me back over the wall and into my car. Although we didn't do a damn thing that night, I felt so confident in my decision to do something. I would never encourage anyone to do some of the things I have chosen to do, but what I have discovered is that feel at my best when I can go to sleep knowing I didn't opt out. My take-a-way is that opting in gives me authentic confidence.

# Consider this:

- What makes you feel brave and confident?

- What is holding you back from standing up for what you believe in?

- How will this knowledge impact your confidence?

what i learned along the way

# 2.9

# BLOOD DRAWS AND JEEP WRANGLERS

Helping Other People Along the Way

**I HAD TO HAVE MY BLOOD DRAWN – NOT SOMETHING I DO VERY OFTEN, BUT WHILE I WAS WAITING IN THE LOBBY, I REMEMBERED, I WAS JUST THERE – NOT TOO LONG AGO.** I had walked into this sterile and bright location and was reminded of my memorable trip here last fall. Last summer was rough health wise, and my doctors were taking extra precautions to make sure I didn't have something else controlling my body. Aliens were out, but an autoimmune disease might have taken over.

Last year, my doctor recommended a long list of tests to the phlebotomist, and as I sat in the chair with a piece of rubber pulling my arm tight, I realized that the woman doing the draw couldn't find a vein. Now, she was all the things you really want in a person holding a needle. She was patient, kind, chatty, yet, all of the sudden, she was ready to give up. After testing out both arms and placing that purple rubber band around my second but equally tiny bicep, she stopped. Then, she looked at me and said, "I'm sorry. I can't do this at all. I am so afraid now, and I don't want to hurt you. I am going to get another tech to take care of this."

In that moment, I looked at her and said, "Absolutely not. If you don't get this blood out of my damn arm, you are going to be a nervous wreck for the next person. Someone has to get blood out of here and it might as well be you." I told her to take a minute, find a big vein and make it happen. She said the obvious next thing. "Are you sure? Are you really sure? I do really need to do this, but I don't want you to be furious because I miss, again." I looked at her with all the confidence in the world and said, "I am definitely sure." even though there was a tiny, little part of me that wasn't. On the second round of first tries, she got it immediately. We were both so relieved, and she said in the kindest tone, "Thank you. I needed that."

It was a little twisted that we were reveling over her getting a needle through my vein, but I realized that while I am working on my own confidence, I am also supposed to be helping people with theirs, too. It's not a competition, and I don't think in any way that there is a supply of confidence that has an end date, a black out date, an expiration date, or that there is a limited supply. In fact, I believe that the world is full of abundance on things like authentic confidence, and since so many people have shared theirs with me, it's about time I pay it forward.

The most important piece that I noticed is that you have to give it away to get it back, and it means taking a risk on people. So many women have shared that they hate to give a genuine compliment to another woman. When you tell a woman she looks great, she will say, "Thanks," or more often, "Oh, this little thing, I just bought this at Target on sale." It is so frustrating, because in the moment of a kindness-transfer, I see women down play themselves.

On top of it, woman tell me consistently that if they give a compliment, they feel like their light shines less than it did before – that in some way giving up a compliment diminishes who they are and for that moment. All the light and attention transfers to the person with whom it is shared. If either of those is not true, then women share that the whole process is just awkward.

Giving a compliment is drastically different than giving confidence. For me, giving confidence is about seeing someone, recognizing what they are tremendous at doing, and giving them a boost in their area of potential growth or current strength. My sweet friend Brandon is a great example.

Brandon and I met at his work – a huge, national car rental chain of all places. When I am not on an airplane traveling, I am usually renting a car two blocks away from home. This guy is amazing at one thing – letting you be on the only thing in his sight. I hate when I am in line for anything like buying tickets to ride at King's Island, ordering a burrito, buying a new iPhone or anything else and the person who is supposed to be helping is distracted. Brandon has the magical power to make you think you are the only person he has to work with that day. It makes my heart happy.

He is consistent, and always screams out a hello to me when I walk in the door. As we grew to know one another, over six months or so, I realized that he is the real deal, and that his eagerness to help is not predicated on some mandatory training. So, we got to talking. We have talked about everything from our favorite country bar to race relations. Yes, we talk about race relations. I am pretty certain this happened after witnessing something or someone at this small office, but it's been too long to know for sure.

Either way, when I asked him about what he wants to do next in this world, he shared all of the opportunities he has in his company. One day, we were talking about how he should move to California because it is so much warmer there, and I told him that some of the cars in LA are stick shifts. I told him he better learn before he gets out there. Now that I think about it, I was probably projecting my want to move to southern CA on him, but regardless, he told me he didn't know how to drive a manual car.

So, I made a promise, and kept my word. One day I showed up early to pick up my rental and asked him if he had a minute to jump in my Jeep. I reminded him that I was on a mission to teach all valets and anyone considering a trip on Amazing Race. You know they always lose in Europe because they can't drive a stick shift.

He was a ringer, and got it immediately, but I upped the ante to make sure he was really getting it right. I made him park, back up and even start on a hill – the stuff that will burn out an engine quickly. I think he stalled it just once, but he got it. For whatever reason, this memory has stuck in my brain like glue. Get it, give it, get it back again, then give it away, again. The smile on my face that day was bigger than his. A simple act of kindness that started with Brandon went through me and right back to him.

My oldest nephew got the chance to learn to drive this old Wrangler, and my act of confidence in him lead him to write a paper about me for school. That paper lead me to want to invest more time with him. When I invest more time in him, I know his confidence grows because I have seen it with my own two eyes.

"Get it, give it, get it back again, then give it away, again."

But, this story does not have a happy ending, because I am reminded of the number of times that I have withheld my confidence in someone, or been unkind in not sharing it. I can count the number of times that I should have spoken up, said something, or pursued with a full heart my certainty in someone else. It is my resolution to not worry about my light all the time. I need not always be a collector, but a giver. This is especially true for women.

Nearly a decade ago, I worked in an office with genuine mean girls. I was an adult with an adult job, but for some reason, I could not connect with this force. I even confronted one of the women, who then placed a post it note on her desk that read: Be kinder. Call it intuition, but eventually after a lot of struggle, I realized I did not, in anyway, want to be friends with these women – even if it meant that my circle of friends at work would be so much smaller. Eventually, I moved to a new company and met incredible women who reintroduced me to the power of female friendships, and the key ingredients of trust, a lot of connecting, and sharing our stories.

What I have realized is that I am already so hard on myself, and my guess is that the same is true for so many other women. My new practice is to be self-aware so that I have time to genuinely and authentically pour into other people, and to remind younger women this is not a competition. I will be mentoring, sponsoring and coaching women. I will be the first to say hello, and I will spend less time in my own head wondering and worrying and more time connecting and supporting. Period.

## Consider this:

- Who needs more confidence from you?

- Where can you give and get confidence? (Siblings, specific friends, mentors, colleagues, supervisor, professor, nieces and nephews or kids, or parents)

- How can you be less of a collector of confidence and more of a giver to other women?

- How does this knowledge impact your confidence?

# what i learned along the way

# 2.10

CAKE AND BROWNIES, BUT NEVER PIZZA AND ICE CREAM!

**I AM GREAT AT BEING A CHAMELEON -** weaving in and out of who I really am to make acquaintances, and especially friends, feel comfortable and happy -- to make sure I connect with each individual who crosses my path. It's tiring and thankless.

Actually, scratch that. I was great at being a chameleon.

Now, I am good at understanding a universal truth: I am not meant to please each and every person I meet. My new favorite saying is: You are not pizza. You can't please everyone. It's true. I am not pizza.

But, you see, I love cake, brownies, pastries, and even doughnuts. I have a secret, though: I don't love ice cream. I am never, ever going to be an ice cream girl. My friends make fun of me relentlessly. They pretend that they are completely aghast that I don't have it as my go-to for every scenario in my life -- think of watching sad movies during that time of the month.

They say things like, "How can you not love ice cream – even on your birthday - for crying out loud?" Then, when they find out I don't drink coffee either their minds are blown. So, I don't love ice cream, and I don't drink coffee. I must come from some dark circle!

But, what I wanted was for everyone to like me. It still irritates me if someone is mad at me, but what doesn't irritate me anymore is when someone doesn't like me. I am working on simplifying my relationships and caring less. This is not about working less, studying less, or being careless. It is about caring less about what other people think of me; and what I've concluded is that I'm not pizza (or ice cream or coffee.) I can't please everyone. Attempting to do so is foolish, reckless and way too much work that will never get accomplished.

"I can't please everyone. Attempting to do so is foolish, reckless and way too much work that will never get accomplished."

I used to place so much stock in a little glare, a snide or sarcastic comment, even a person who didn't want to be my pair in a group discussion. A bad evaluation could take me out of my game for weeks. I distinctly remember being asked to work on a project for my favorite client. My co-facilitator and I spent months working on brand new curriculum, and then we presented, entertained, told stories, and delivered some of our best work for three days straight. At the end of the project, we sat in the lobby bar going through 300 evaluations. Two hundred and ninety nine of them were neutral, constructive, and even fabulous. But, one of them said, "Erin Fischer, you think you are funny, and you are not funny at all."

To this day, I think I could probably pick this person out in a lineup. It's been at least five years since that day, but I am certain I know who it is! Regardless, I let this young woman take up space in my head for two weeks; it knocked my confidence upside down. I remember being so conscious of myself - feeling so hurt, and wondering if I was a fraud. I was getting paid to do something very specific. Present, train, develop – be a speaker. What if I was really bad at what I was getting a check every two weeks to do?

Now that I have some distance from this, it is easy to see how I got in my head. The pain was quick and relentless, and I have no doubt that it was valid, but now, I think very differently.  First, I play the law of averages. After speaking to over 18,000 people in my career, there is bound to be someone who does not like my message. Even the most revered people have critics. Brene Brown, Elizabeth Gilbert, and even Glennon Doyle Melton talk about their faultfinders and decriers. Second, I worry a lot more about my own evaluation of my work than I do of the evaluation of the people in my audience.  After I get off stage, I am dedicated to reflecting on my product, my ability to connect, and my story telling (did I get to the point and was I clever). It is not about being careless, for me it is about caring less – about what everyone else thinks.

So, let me be clear. Pizza is truly amazing, and I would eat it every day. Ice cream is amazing, too, but that doesn't mean it is for me. Ice cream isn't sitting around, moping, and being sad because I don't like it. Ice cream simply doesn't care. Like ice cream, I am not for everyone.

I may be awesome, but I have learned a hard lesson. Just because I care, just because I work hard, just because I am kind and thoughtful doesn't give me a special power. Just because I am a great friend, a great listener, and a great lunch date, doesn't mean that everyone wants to be my best friend. Just because I write amazing curriculum, deliver a funny and heart-warming keynote, and am very thorough with my clients doesn't mean I am going to get every contract, a perfect five star evaluation, or that every person in my audience will love my work.

Now, my confidence comes from a place of authenticity. I don't have to play games, pretend to be someone I am not, put on a fake persona, or do anything else insincere; and I don't spend time being a chameleon. I spend my time being a better human being and owning the power to go to bed each night with a grateful heart – and dreams of cake and brownies.

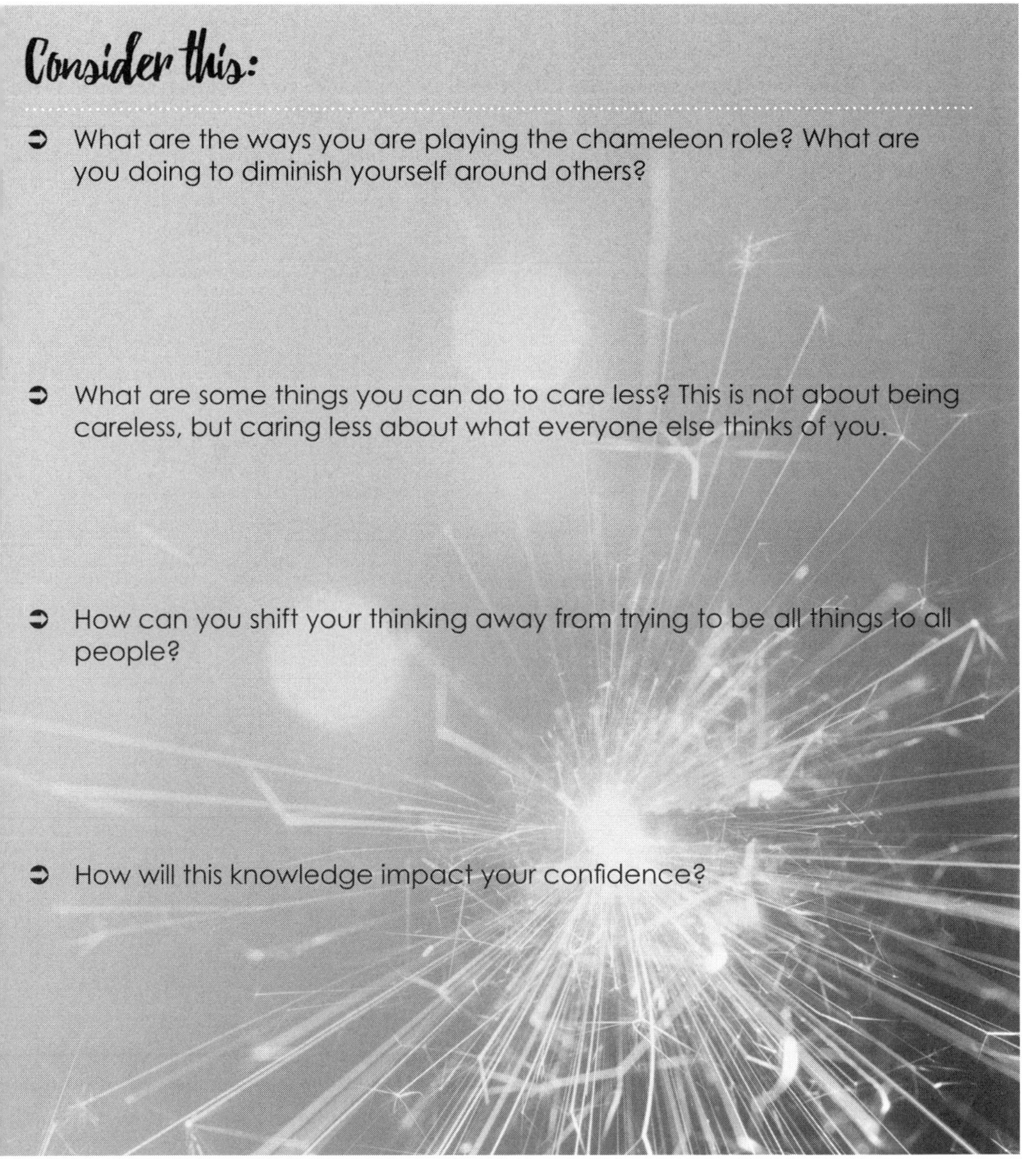

## Consider this:

- What are the ways you are playing the chameleon role? What are you doing to diminish yourself around others?

- What are some things you can do to care less? This is not about being careless, but caring less about what everyone else thinks of you.

- How can you shift your thinking away from trying to be all things to all people?

- How will this knowledge impact your confidence?

# what i learned along the way

# 2.11

## THE DOCTOR'S OFFICE IS A TEST

*Sticking Up for Myself*

**I DECIDED TO BECOME AN ADVOCATE FOR MY HUSBAND'S HEALTH LAST YEAR.** I was tired of different doctors prescribing medication for him that didn't work. We had a great physician who went out of business and as a result, my husband was going to a new doctor that didn't have the full picture of his health history.

He was being put on medication that was having an adverse reaction to his body, and this had to stop. On top of it, he was battling his second, self-proclaimed man-cold. Trust me, they can be devastating to an entire family!

As a result, I called our original physician, who had just gone back into business, after two years, in another part of town. I did two things during a call to his office that I rarely do. First, I was really transparent with the nurse about what was going on with my husband. My belief, even though untrue, was that nurses had heard it all. Therefore, she didn't want some other person complaining about another ailment. Yet ironically, my vulnerability got her on board with me. I was still kind, but I opened up and gave her the full picture.

In my head, I was replaying the commercials that play on TV that show a patient with all sorts of health concerns, then when they pan to the doctor's office and the physician says,"Do you have anything else you want to discuss?" the patient is silent. I was tired of being silent. She could tell this was important to me and that I wasn't droning on without a purpose. As a result, I could tell she knew this had to be a priority.

Then, I said to her, "I want a full hour of the doctor's time on Monday." Without hesitation, she said, "I have you booked from 1:10 p.m. until 2 p.m. Get here early and get your paperwork done and we can squeeze in another ten minutes."

I asked for what I wanted and I got it, but why did I wait to advocate for him for so long? This has been going on for years. I could scream looking back at the number of times that we were told to "try" something out and see how it works. I could spit looking back at the number of times we were told to come in for another 10-minute appointment and no action was taken, and I could count the number of times that I was frustrated, my husband was desperate and we were stuck on the roller coaster of health care. My limiting beliefs said to me things like, "Let the doctor do his work. Things won't always go your way. No body gets a longer appointment than 10 to 15 minutes."

But that is not true. Sometimes, when you confidently ask for what you really want or need, you get it.

> "Sometimes, when you confidently ask for what you really want or need, you get it."

At the beginning of May, a year ago, I found myself at an orthopedic doctor's office after discovering that I had a frozen shoulder. It has been five months of little sleep and rounds of physical therapy. By the way,

Physical therapy offices should really be on reality TV. Are you kidding me? The things you see and hear are hysterical, and there is more complaining by grown adults in PT, than by little kids who have walked for more than 15 minutes and are so tired.

After an obnoxiously loud MRI, the doctor found little adhesions attached to my shoulder. A frozen shoulder at age 38 was not what anyone expected, but there it, was slowing me down. I couldn't even put my sweater on, and I couldn't raise my arms to shave my armpits. Gross. These tiny little adhesions stuck to my body were doing a number on my daily life.

So, I waited in the doctor's huge reception area, and I was finally escorted back to an exam room. The nurse was brand new and had no idea what was going on or what to do. I wanted to tell her to be confident ever since my feeling of what this team could accomplish was going down the drain with every one of her indecisions, but I didn't. Personal self-awareness is great, but I was not on a mission to facilitate a conversation about confidence, that day.

The nurse did all of the obligatory things on her nurse checklist. She took my blood pressure, my temperature, and then she asked a series of questions like: Tell me what is going on with you? Before she left, she said to me, "Please take off your top and put on this gown so the doctor can examine your arm."

In this brief, awkward moment, I had two choices. I could be the old Erin and oblige or be the new Erin and simply say no. I quickly thought, "I haven't met this doctor and there is no way I am getting undressed before I meet him. This is absurd to think that he should see me with half of my clothes off before he even knows my name." So, I looked at the nurse and said, "I will wait. I want to meet the doctor, first. There is no need to get undressed, yet." She was stunned, and I think, secretly, a bit proud.

I am certain there is a significant amount of research about what happens to patients when they feel strange about something going on with their body and are afraid to speak up, and I am also certain there is even more research about what happens when a patient is put in an even more uncomfortable position by being half naked while trying to describe chronic pain, a sustained injury or an embarrassing ailment. When you have to get naked on top of it, it's just too much.

In this moment, I didn't give a damn about following the traditional, simple rule: Do what is asked of you – especially when someone of authority says so. I cared more about being an advocate for my own body - using all the confidence I could to talk though my issue, while keeping my clothes on. I was craving being an advocate for my own health. Remember, I hadn't slept through the night in five months. I would wake up every 45 minutes in pain and have to shift my body around to find the perfect place to rest. I hope that this confidence was not coming from exhaustion, rather a place of personal buoyancy, but whatever was driving this moment was very liberating.

I was not going to take my shirt off and put on a gown that made me feel less than confident just to appease someone who was told that is the protocol. So, I didn't. But like every life lesson for the past several months, I knew some little tiny thing inside of me was beginning to change.

I don't think I will ever be a mean and nasty, nor do I want to be. But, I want to have less regret in the areas that make up my life. It is the tiny, daily decisions between yes and no, or yes, but not right now. Then, there is also this layer of no – hell no!

The irony is that the doctor never asked me to put on that gown. I sat with him for more than 15 minutes, and he never needed to see my perfectly shaved armpit and brightly colored purple bra. (Yes, we all do these things when we go to the doctor for fear of being judged!) During this time, I even made him laugh. He asked me what I did and I shared with him that I am a professional speaker. The credibility that I have as a human being impacts how other people treat me. I want to be treated like I am a precious commodity and that my body, my current pain, and my treatment are necessary. I didn't want my shyness to dictate how aggressive he could be when treating something that was destroying my daily routines.

So, I chose to stay dressed and made a recording in my brain that screamed: Do what is right for you. Don't forget the doctor's office is always a test.

# Consider this:

- Where do you need to advocate for yourself? (The doctor's office, work, school, or some place else?)

- What do you need and how can you ask for it?

- How will this knowledge impact your confidence?

# what i learned along the way

# 2.12

## REVIEW AND REGRET

**ONE OF MY BIGGEST CONCERNS IN LIFE RIGHT NOW IS THE STATE OF COLLEGE WOMEN ACROSS AMERICA.** I want to take so many of them home with me – to love on them, and to build their confidence. They are struggling. They are brilliant, smart, funny, and interesting, but many of them are struggling. I think part of it is their age, but part of it is the intense pressure they put on themselves.

At the beginning of my confidence keynote, I use Simon Sinek's technique on starting with "Why." I open with the question, "Why do we need confidence now more than ever?" The women share that the media has an impact, but also that they are in transition and need real jobs in the next few years which require fabulous interviewing skills. They add that they are vulnerable, need to find happiness – the answers run the gamut. But, later on, when I ask them about the things that get in the way, they are reticent, almost sad for a few moments about the state of their own beliefs, and then I circle back. "So, what is getting in the way of real confidence?"

Consistently, they say one stunning thing. At the end of each evening, they review their day from top to bottom. They think about each conversation, wondering, what if, and they think about each interaction, wondering what they could have said or done differently. It is heartbreaking every time I hear it.

We all have regrets. My God, my list is long. Very long. I think of things I wish I had done differently, in particular, that would have been more thoughtful or more servant-leadership like, but a review each day seems beyond exhausting to consider.

Reviewing each day, each hour, each conversation and each interaction to line up the regrets, sorrows, misgivings and compunctions is a silent mind disease. If one or two women out of 300 did this, I would play the law of averages, but when 90% of women raise their hand when asked if "they are in the same boat, "I began to wonder. Why are we so hard on ourselves? Out of 300 women in a keynote, 90% of the women are reflecting on their actions in a negative way. Furthermore, I know this takes a toll on confidence and stress hormones.

I think confidence comes from learning, trying, failing miserably and succeeding again, but there are some bad habits that get in the way of trying and failing just for the learning opportunity. Being too hard on myself is at the top of that list. I too have been in the injudicious cycle of review and regret sometimes.

I do not believe in perfection, but I do expect a lot of myself. I keep reflecting on this and wondering if it comes from a place of being a high achiever, or the need to people please, but beyond review and regret, what am I secretly craving is a huge leap. I am in desperate need for a big, gigantic, scary, fast-forward wild leap. I want to feel something even if it is regret. I want to have the confidence to be bold and brave even if it means I have a wild failure. I will own that my privilege allows for this window of hurdling myself into something brand new, but I keep debating the risk between the two types of regret, the first comes from failing (review and regret), and the second comes from not trying to fail (giant leap for new knowledge and experience).

I don't wait to fail, that sounds miserable, but I have this strong, fierce push to explore and make unknown, or even unreliable, choices to questions I have not even pondered. One of my friends Kara described this to me a few years ago. She was telling me about her only daughter and how much she adored this creature in her life. As Kara and I were sharing tea, she said the most brilliant thing about her experience. "I wanted to see what this body can really do. It's like taking a car out on the highway and letting it go – letting it unleash. My body is beyond amazing and I wanted to see how it could really perform. I wanted a baby, but I also wanted to test my body to see what it was capable of doing."

That's what I want. I want to get out on the road and start revving up my soul, again. I want to do something new and not be so damn afraid of the review and regret. Now, I know with certainty, I do not want to have a child, but I have dreams of a second business that allows me to support other small business owners through a co-working space. I have been sitting on this thing for 2 ½ years because I am so afraid to fail. I have looked at spaces, toured a dozen other co-working spaces, talked to multiple commercial agents, and even put a business plan together.

So, there it all is, tied up in a bow, and then I reflect again. I am afraid hurt will happen. What if I am not enough, what if I have a huge blind spot, what if it doesn't work and it hurts. What if it hurts me, anyone I love, or anyone who is investing in me? It's not just the business side; it's the mental game, too.

So, why does Mark Twain say, "Twenty years from now you will be more disappointed by the things you didn't do than by the ones you did do."? In fact, I should be asking myself not just what I don't want to regret, but what do I want to do that makes me feel alive.

A reminder hit my inbox. Experience breeds confidence. I had it wrong for a long time. I always thought confidence came first, but in fact, experience, mastery, failing, trying, experimenting – that's the stuff that breeds my natural, authentic confidence. It's like exercise – pain before gain. Actually, it's like giving up caffeine. For two weeks, your whole body feels like it is going to explode. Then, on day 15, something magical happens. You feel a million times lighter; less tired, and ironically have more focus. All of that giving up in order to gain.

I have learned that exposure comes with regrets, but also big rewards. So, I am going to be mindful to tell other women, who only see my finished project, about the other side that is filled with trial and error, not a perfect plan. And I am going to spend less time in regret and more time in experiencing all of it.

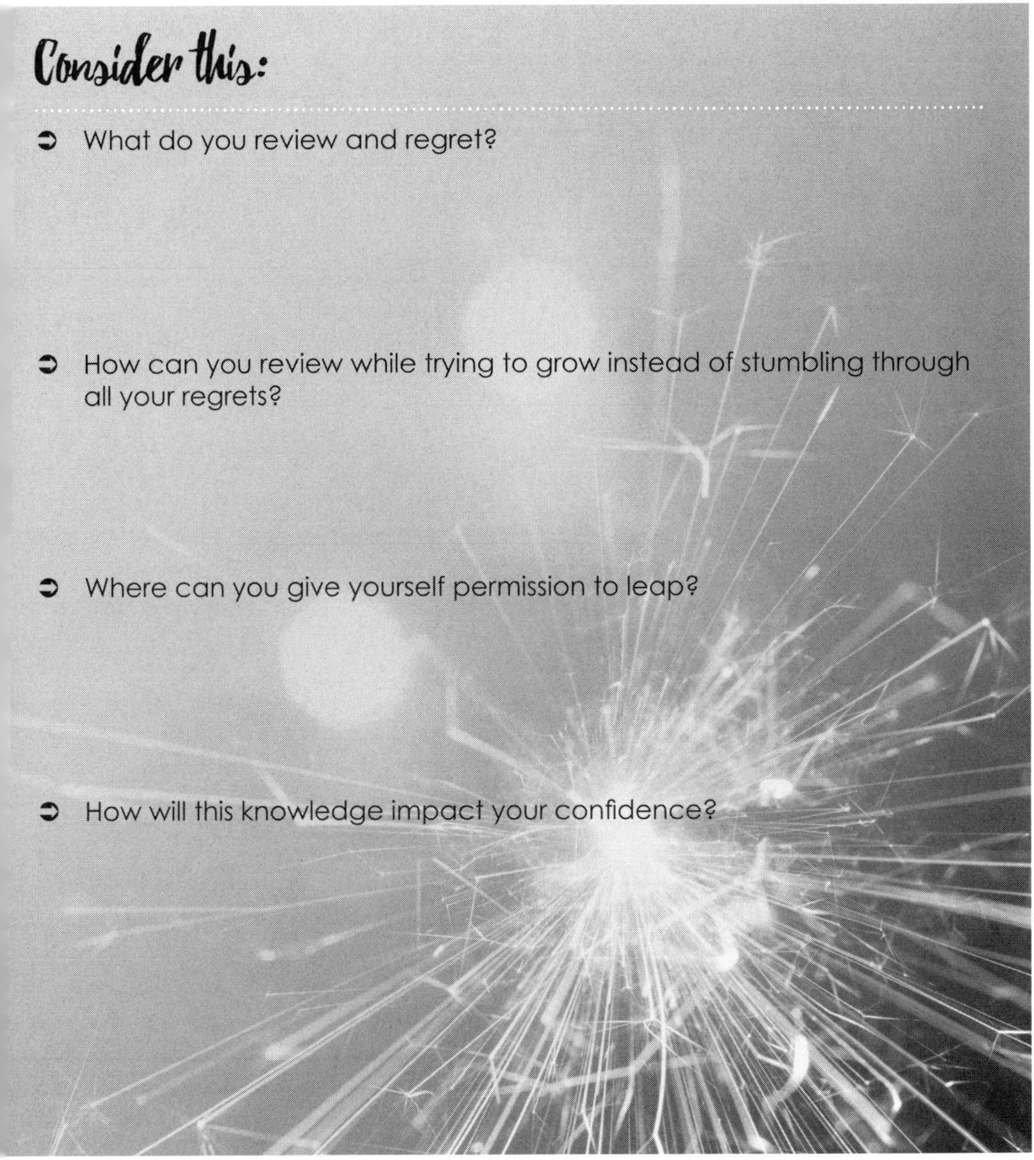

## Consider this:

- What do you review and regret?

- How can you review while trying to grow instead of stumbling through all your regrets?

- Where can you give yourself permission to leap?

- How will this knowledge impact your confidence?

# what i learned along the way

# 2.13

RETURN THE TOMATO BREAD

**IN MY HEAD, I AM THINKING, "HE COUGHED ON THE TOMATO BREAD. WHAT THE HELL?"** He – our waiter - stood in our section of El Nacional in Barcelona for 15 minutes completely ignoring the fact that we were seated at one his tables. Now, he has just coughed on our food. Our tomato bread - to be exact.

As we ordered, he looked at every other person walking by our tapas restaurant while my sweet mom ordered a cheese platter, prosciutto, stuffed eggs, three Estrellas and a glass of red wine. *"Look at my mother when she orders."* I tried to implore him with my body language, but he never looked at her. Not once. We all laughed that it was unlikely that he would get any of our order right, but in fact, by some miracle, it all came out properly - until the tomato bread.

We assumed one of two things. Tomato bread would be either brightly colored bruschetta or bread with Spanish cheese and tomatoes baked in focaccia. We were wrong on both accounts, and surprised when we got bread in a basket with real tomatoes right off the vine. When in Spain, right? So, we cut our tomatoes, salted them and ate them as part of our meal that early evening.

But right before this tomato bread arrived, I witnessed this creature of a server cough on our bread. It was a closed mouth cough, but it was right on the two black baskets that accompanied our bread, and well, our tomatoes.

Maybe it was the fatigue after a six-hour time change coupled with long sightseeing days that included walking tens of thousands of steps through thousand-year-old cities. But it was also a fear of conflict. My mother hates it, my husband dreads it, and my father, who doesn't mind speaking his piece didn't witness this. So, I let it go.

I want to say this essential part again. I let it go. The bread-coughing incident? I let it go.

Foolishly and regretfully, I let a man cough on our bread without stopping him, addressing him, or, most importantly, demanding that he return our tomatoes and bread for new ones. As I write, I am reminded of a simple server rule: He may have returned from the kitchen with the same exact food. However, my personal right to self-respect was declined the minute I didn't have the confidence to speak up.

In fairness, I have sent food back before, and complained about egregious service in my life. I give credit to the Food Channel for this. I know how my salmon is supposed to be cooked, now - a sear on both sides and delicately perfect in the middle.

Even from my past experiences, I know that one force or many collective things can impact my confidence to stand up for little, but annoying things like the right to cough-free tomato bread in Spain.

These factors most certainly include people. I learn the tolerance of other people and act accordingly. What I can do and say in front of my grandmother is very different than what I can do and say in front of a cousin or a sister-in-law. The way I act in front of my parents can be in sharp contrast to the way I handle things in front of my siblings. A mentor, a boss , or a client can change my confidence level instantly.

I am great at assessing each situation and trying to determine the weight of my need to raise my voice for what is right. Will a neighbor see me at the farmer's market, or do I really care if the cashier at the grocery store is annoyed because I don't want to buy Cotton Candy grapes now at $42 a pound, even after they have been in my cart? (Yes, they do exist, and yes, they are amazing, and yes $42 a pound is a wee bit of an exaggeration.)

What I have learned is that I need to raise my level of consciousness around the factors and forces impacting my confidence in order to handle things like returning tomato bread after it has been coughed on. I also learned confidence comes and goes, and my fatigue has a great deal to do with that.

Here are some of the other things I learned.

| THE FORCES THAT IMPACT MY CONFIDENCE |
|---|
| ♦ Perceived age of someone. (It's much easer to have confidence with my six year old nephew than a CEO.) |
| ♦ Perceived experience of someone. (It's much easier when my resume is longer.) |
| ♦ Perceived level of their confidence. (Too pretty, too smart, too confident? That can throw off my confidence.) |
| ♦ Perceived ability to recommend me/my work to other people. (It's much easier to prove myself when I don't need your approval.) |
| ♦ How hungry, tired, angry I am (Being hangry or tangry has a huge impact.) |
| ♦ How much I have been hurt and am willing to stand up for myself (It's much easier to have confidence when the stakes are low.) |
| ♦ How much I need to maintain a current relationship. |
| ♦ How much I am willing to try to impress someone. |

What I have noticed is that subconsciously, I am constantly accounting for all of these things, which by the way, can be very exhausting, but my mindfulness around these forces started to impact the way I showed up. Now, I am just trying to show up as me – the same person every time – with a little more or little less cussing depending on who is in the room!

## Consider this:

- What are some of the things you are avoiding because of your confidence level?

- What are some of the things you can let go along the way?

- What are some of the good and bad forces that have an impact on your confidence?

- How can you become more conscious of these forces?

- How will this knowledge impact your confidence?

# what i learned along the way

# 2.14

## MIND THE RECORDER

Practicing Self Awareness

**ONE OF MY MENTORS, CARLA, TOLD ME TO MIND MY RECORDER.** To give some more context, she shared this with me when I was going through a particularly dark time with a lot of revolving hurt in my life. I distinctly remember calling her on the way home one day – all while trying not to cry and lose it. Her advice was to mind what was in my mind. She told me that people are good at repeating things in our day to day life not because we are foolish, stupid or silly, or that we are gluttons for punishment, but because we are good at hitting rewind to find something that feels familiar and replaying it over and over. Good or bad.

At the time, I was good at replaying being nice, for the sake of zero disruption, and at almost any cost. In tough situations, I held onto friendships, often too afraid to debate someone or stick up for myself because I didn't want to lose anyone. I would suck it up, swallow my raw emotions and let a lot go. I think letting things go has a unique power unto itself, but not at the expensive habit of being unhappy. There were a lot of times that I was unhappy because I was hitting replay, and more importantly, not being an active participant in my own choices.

Then, something happened. Over the past two years, I pushed back on three major relationships in my life, and started to set a new recording. I told one of my dearest friends that she hurt me like hell, and that her actions led to a lot of tough things that impacted my job in a very direct way. I told her that I was mad and disappointed. We never once raised our voices in our multiple discussions over four months, but I got really clear about what I was "supposed" to do to be nice and what I needed to do to protect my own self-worth and personal integrity. We missed several birthdays and holidays, and I missed her kids growing up for a period of time, but what came out of these tough conversations was shocking.

For the first time, we both stopped pretending that nice was the way to act like a lady, and pursued two really invaluable conversations over a few days. She shared with me the things that I did that hurt her like hell, too. The first share was the hardest but most important. I didn't stay at the funeral after her dad passed away suddenly. I went to the funeral and the burial site, but I didn't stay at their church to console her after her father was buried on the coldest day on record. At the time, I had an excuse – our mutual friend was in from out of town to go to the funeral and needed to get back, but really it was just an excuse. I should have gone to that church, ate little finger foods, and hugged her family, but more importantly, I should have been standing by her side when she couldn't stand up anymore. I made a huge mistake, and when we both got real, I could genuinely apologize for my regrettable choice.

Then, I discovered that our friendship had a lot of value to her. She is not one to jump on the phone, and because of her busy life, she is not the social coordinator, but I let those perceived indicators indicate of our relationship's value. While playing nice, I never addressed that frustration and lack of connection. While playing nice, I never set expectations or talked through what I needed. Again, our recorders said, "Keep the peace, be agreeable, don't ruffle anyone's feathers, don't raise your voice, and don't ask for what you want because you might lose what you have." As a woman, I realize I am not alone in this.

My recorder has some other bad plays, too. When I was younger, it said not to break up with a guy, not to ask for a job, much less a promotion, not to be confrontational or do something that will make you stand out (other than hard work.) Some of my recorder is strong and fierce, and makes me who I am today, but some of my recorder has some updating to do. The work to make it happen is so hard because it means overriding my natural tendencies to make change, and it means that I have to give up on previous, once normal, thoughts and replace them with something brand new. Stretching hurts.

Right now, I am working on updating my recorder when it comes to handling unpleasant conversations. I just sent an e-mail to a prospect saying that I would not offer wholesale prices for my work, meaning I would not discount the fee that my clients currently pay for me to speak. My fee is my fee. I thank my sales coach for that new recording, but I always worry what it means when I say no to someone. I am working on telling my family members that I love them, but I don't believe some of their political opinions. I am working on telling my husband that date night is still really important, even though we are both so busy, and both need our own down time. I am working on telling another family member that she can't make me choose sides, and that I have a lot of love in my heart to share, but I get to make the decision on who I spend time with, not her.

For a long time, my recording said it would be impossible to write a first book or even a second book; it said that I couldn't start a second business or that I would never make the money that I wanted to make – so I could travel the world. Yet, all of these things proved to be wrong.

My recorder has told me which job titles I can have, or how much money I can ask for, and which project I can handle. I do have limits, but my recorder was setting limits instead of my logic.

Then, my talented colleagues who sit with me on a board that serves women leadership educators reminded me of a few things women face. First, many of us believe we are impostors. Dr. Pauline Rose Clance talks about this in her work centered on the Impostor Phenomenon. She argues that women tend to think everything they get is by chance, fluke or luck. Got a good grade, the job you applied for and really wanted, and the partner of your dreams? It happened by chance, not hard work.

Then, many women feel like they are in a place of having to be effortlessly perfect. Effortless perfectionism is a new trend to me, but it is compelling to discuss and forceful to manage. It is the sense that women need to show up looking perfect, dressing perfectly, and acting/presenting/sharing/delivering perfection – an impossibility. Right now, we also know that from the Anxiety and Depression Association of America that 40 million adults are suffering from anxiety and depression. So, not only are we dealing with confidence, but we are also dealing with these major forces. Anxiety, impostor phenomenon, and effortless perfectionism are on the list, plus, rumination, mean girls, and women not having a coach, mentor or sponsor.

What I have learned is that if my recorder is filled with healthy recordings, I can thrive, but it is impossible to think that I have led a perfect life. I have an incredible family, but they are not the only influences on my recordings. I have witnessed so much in my years. So again, the lesson for me is mindfulness. I am focusing on being mindful in and around:

1. The way I treat people I already love! (Do I give them my best, even when I am at my worst? It's easy to give less to people who are already fully invested in me, but it is so unfair.)
2. The way I treat people who are new to my life. (Do I let them in, do I give them access to all of the sides of me, including my vulnerable side, and do I seek to understand them fully, in return?)
3. The way that I am conscious of being brave and taking leaps even when it means I may be exposed to hurt. (Do I take leaps and show other women the unfinished side of me?)
4. The way I need to overcome my stop sign thinking. The thinking that gives easily affords me the easy out because I can't immediately see the solution. (Do I look for option C or avoid stop sign thinking?)
5. The way I need to envision around new recordings. I need to practice replacing my crappy stuff before I hit rewind and play. (Do I consciously consider my thoughts and actions?)

So, on the list of things to mind, I am putting this at the top. Healthy recording sessions.

"What I have learned is that if my recorder is filled with healthy recordings, I can thrive, but it is impossible to think that I have lead a perfect life."

## Consider this:

- What can you do to pay attention to your recorder more?

- What are the top three brilliant things your recorder tells you? What are the top three not-so-brilliant things your recorder tells you?

- What do you need to record over? What needs a new look?

- What else do you need to be mindful of for you and other women?

- How will this knowledge impact your confidence?

# what i learned along the way

# 2.15

## CRAZY BUSY IS NOT AWESOME

**I HAVE BECOME REALLY CLOSE TO A EXTENDED FAMILY MEMBER WHO HAS TURNED INTO A GREAT FRIEND.** She is wickedly smart, has raised beautiful children, and from the outside, she has her life together.

When I call her to catch up, we start with the usual pleasantries like any catch up phone call. "Hey, how are you guys doing? What's new in your world? How are the kids?" I ask. Every time I wait in anticipation for her common and perfunctory response. I even get a little giggle now because she says the same thing. "We are so crazy busy. I mean between the kids school, sports, my husband's job, my job, a new house, the new dog....." The list goes on and on and on. No matter why, she is always "crazy busy."

She is and has always been crazy busy, and she is not alone. So many of my conversations with my girlfriends start with this silly routine. They list all the things that are making them crazy busy, and then I reciprocate. But now I get stuck because I have this new level of self-awareness around it. Am I supposed to sympathize, apologize, or give advice? Hell, I don't know, but I know that it makes me feel something really weird. These chitchat openers give me the sense that my life is just not as important or elevated because my list just isn't as long.

Regretfully, I must admit that I have been pushing the long-list-agenda with all my friends and colleagues. I have started casual conversations with my laundry list of the things that make me exhausted and overwhelmed.

Then, I had a little 'aha' moment. I realized that I am running a race with no ending point. I have traveled all across the United States this year, and I have traversed roughly 103,000 miles on flights, delivered dozens of projects and keynotes, built my business by 20% in the second year, and have a phenomenal social life – when I am in town. But I had a mindset that busy meant productive. I had a mindset that busy meant important, and I had a mindset that the more I shared about how busy I am the better I would feel.

Crazy busy = a long list, and a long list = an important life. Or so I thought.

I finally came to the simple conclusion that I am not that important. Well, I am important to my 94-year-old Grandma. Just ask her. My conclusion is that I am average, despite winning a contest at my elementary school for the best quote about friendship. I won for saying, "Everyone is special and so am I." What? Who let me think that?

Last week I got some more clarity. I was with a member of a client team, and we were working on how to address the mental health issues of men on college campuses. Through our discussion, one gentleman sweetly shared with me that his wife told him he was average. Average. Nothing special. Lovely, but not out of this world. I processed that comment for a few hours while I was running a brainstorming session, and at lunch, when I sat next to him, I asked him if he could give me some context around her thought process. Was she like me trying to temper my husband's self-perceived awesomeness, too? You know the one that can sell millions of dollars for his company, but certainly can't find his way around a kitchen to make a home cooked meal.

But Scott said something brilliant. His wife's comment was actually validation – a compliment of sorts. It was to say, "You are just fine. Being average is the place to be, friend." He said it took all sorts of pressure off of him to be exemplary all the time. He also shared that it decreased his stress and anxiety when things in life didn't always go according to plan. He said that being average let him breathe and be normal. It's all I could ever hope for – to be normal, even in a land where everyone is supposed to be special.

Being normal then, means I can't start conversations off being above normal while giving my long list of woes and things that make my life hectic. It's like I was running the Annual Crazy Busy Race, and I wasn't told that there wasn't a finish line, a medal, a prize or even a tracker. You know those little devices they put on your shoe to see how far and fast you have made it. There is no race, yet I have been running it. I know the real pain and hurt of running the crazy busy race – exhaustion, frustration, feeling helpless, and always in competition.

"It's all I could ever hope for - to be normal, even in a land where everyone is supposed to be special."

Sometimes, I have even been a martyr after running the damn race, and being irritated for not knowing the rules. Other times, I have been the gal handing out the water encouraging everyone to keep running. Both seem ridiculous now.

I will either choose to be crazy busy or I will choose to be normal, average and healthy. I have learned that these things have more value, but are not accepted, yet. I am proud of the women who I know who are secretly getting out of the race, and don't have to share their daily victory of exhaustion anymore.

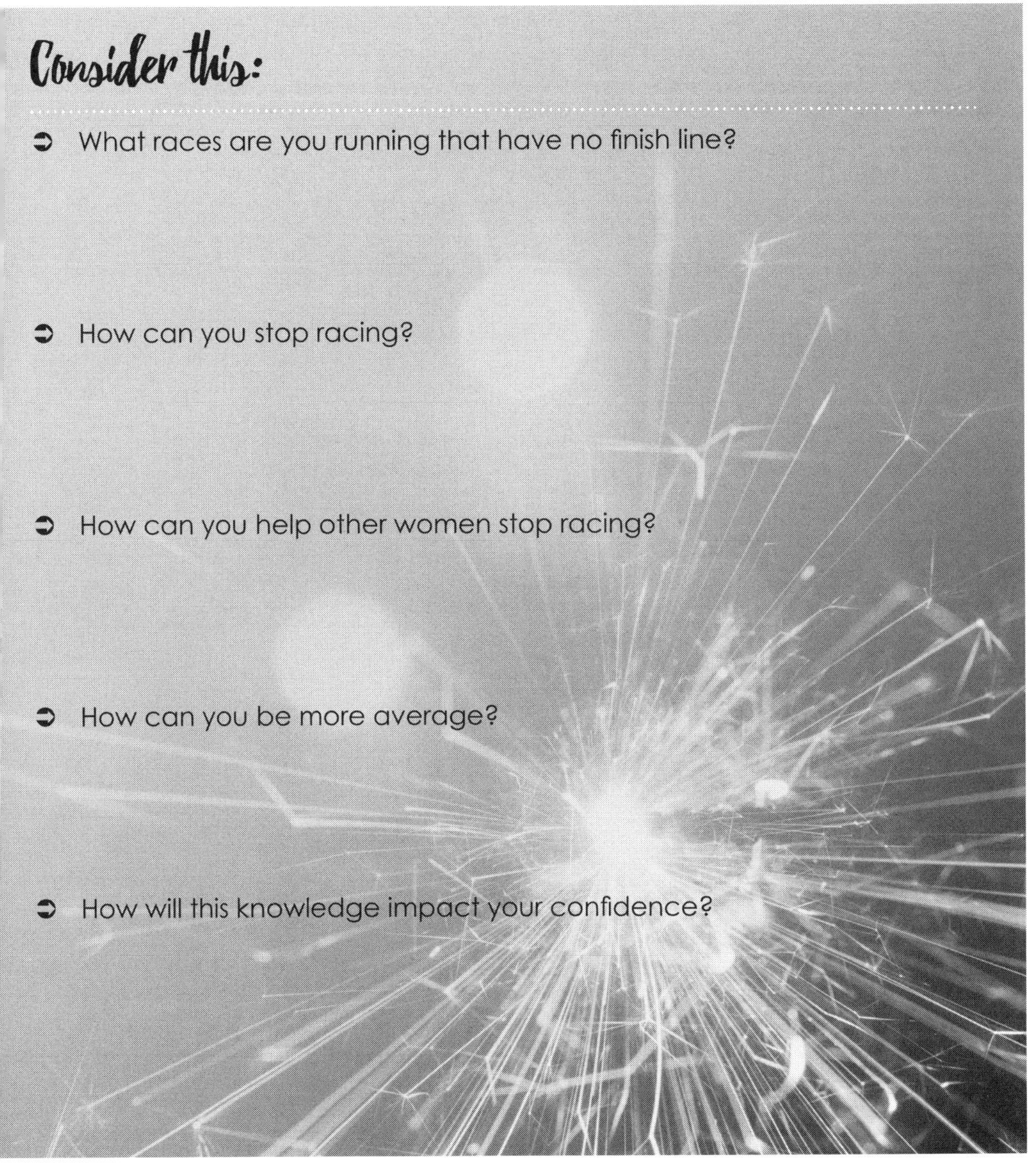

## Consider this:

- What races are you running that have no finish line?

- How can you stop racing?

- How can you help other women stop racing?

- How can you be more average?

- How will this knowledge impact your confidence?

# 2.16

## BEING SOLAR POWERED

**A FEW YEARS AGO, I WAS VOLUNTEERING FOR A WEEK TO SERVE COLLEGE STUDENTS DURING A LEADERSHIP RETREAT.** It was six days in a beautiful center that once was a family home for a wealthy banker from the Chicago area. To say it is gorgeous is an understatement. It sits on hundreds of acres and boasts dozens of gargantuan bedrooms, marble bathrooms, and a mighty view that is stunning.

What I loved and still love about this remote location is all the outdoor space. It feels like I am getting the free, but really powerful, force of nature to help slow my body down. During every single break, I would sneak outside to sit in the sun and soak in the lake and the thousands of deciduous trees, and my favorite – the evergreens. I would eat lunch without dessert without an extra moment of lingering, so I could get back to the view.

On the first day of faculty training, we were assigned a little space for our small group of 10 students. We were to meet in this space two or three times a day for a few hours at a time. We all took a guided tour of the main house, and along the way we were assigned a room. I was assigned the basement. A beautiful, well-appointed basement, albeit, but a basement. I detest basements – primarily because they have no windows and smell funny – even when they have pool tables and fancy wood on the wall.

For some reason, I was brave enough to actually say, "Will anyone trade me, please?" One kind soul, a woman in her 60s looked at me and said, "Sure thing." I justified my request and said, "I just don't think I can be here in this basement for the next few days. I need the sun."

Then, she made the observation that completely described me. She leaned over and whispered, "You must be solar powered." YES! It's true, I never thought about it before, but I am solar powered. No one has ever mentioned those words to me, but I know I am a mess in the month of February. The holidays are gone, the days are still too short, and it feels too long before April and May – my favorite months of the year. She was right. I crave the sun, not in the way a 80s Copper Tone Tan model might crave the sun, but in the way that it makes me feel like breathing happiness into my body.

Being outside – in the sun, well, that's my flow activity – the kind of activity that brings me joy. It's like surfing for Hawaiians, or skiing for Coloradans, or riding a motorcycle for Harley lovers, or dancing to Hip Hop for New Yorkers, or being at the beach for Floridians – they just have to do it because it makes them feel so damn good. My Dad rides 2,500 miles a year on his bike, my Mom reads dozens of books a year, my niece Kaleigh loves being in plays, my nephew Kyle loves working out, my husband loves playing golf, all my sisters-in-law love drinking wine, and my Grandma, well she is a stock market genius at 94 years of age.

If I am having a really bad day, there is one thing that tops all other flow activities for me. I wish I could say it was something metaphysical like Yoga or meditation, but it's not. It's riding around in my Jeep Wrangler with the top off and the music blaring. For some magical reason, which I can't explain, I can get out of any mood when I am in my '03, rusted out Wrangler. I listen to 90s rap music, and I am transported out of my body into a place where my brain can't over think or over process – it just does. It does whatever brains are supposed to do when they are repairing themselves after becoming fragmented, tired and disjointed. My brain goes into recovery mode and restores and realigns.

For some reason, that I desperately pray a scientist will explain to me, I get re-centered when I find I am in my flow. I can feel unrestrained joy, and of course a surge of confidence in myself. It feels like a whisper of someone saying, "It will all be just fine." The second thing I have discovered is that accomplishing something really hard always does the trick, too.

"I can feel unrestrained joy, and of course a surge of confidence in myself. It feels like a whisper of someone saying, 'It will all be just fine.'"

When I set out to write my first book, I instinctively knew it was possible, but I didn't have the map right away. I struggled with the number of rounds of edits from all of the collaborating writers, an editor who was having a hard time with technology, a designer who was in Asia for two weeks in the middle of my design timeline, and a few other interesting little items, but when I got the first shipment of books in the mail, I breathed this really heavy breath of contentment. Damn. I figured it out. Unlocking puzzle pieces, doing something that challenges my brain to deconstruct and reconstruct, or accomplishing something that someone told me I couldn't do based on any number of restrictions makes me wild with experiential confidence.

Finally, I have learned that helping other people find their flow makes me feel wildly confident, too.  While on a service immersion trip to Hawaii, I was tasked with creating a schedule of environmental service projects for one of my clients. I knew that we had a limited number of days on Oahu, but I also knew that building bonds with a community is an invaluable payoff in a future that also includes dingy bunk beds and a tight 15 passenger van. So, I booked us on a double decker ropes course. One of our students traversed the gigantic rope ladder, and by ladder, I mean rope jungle gym! She hooked in on the top deck, and made her first few moves, but the height of the entire structure got to her, and she asked to get down. I was riddled with so much regret for being more focused on my own journey than hers. So, after a few days, I asked the camp staff if the two of us could get back up there. The camp was kind enough to agree, and thankfully so was she. We decided on a different challenge – the Tango Tower.

For an hour or so, we climbed up this apparatus that was just as high and just as challenging. She whined and complained and was genuinely scared, but I was not ever going to give up on her. For some reason, my gut said she had to do this.

As she slowly made it to the top, she started getting her voice back. She started making confident decisions about where she was moving to next. She was actually being strategic. Then, she got to the very top level all by herself.

As she sat up on the ledge, 25 feet in the air, she overlooked the vast Pacific Ocean and started to cry. I hugged her as tight as I have ever hugged someone when we both got down to the ground. Then, she shared something to me that made me feel an emotion I had never felt. She looked at me and said, "No one has ever pushed me before. No one has ever challenged me or pushed me through something like this. My dad is blind and as a result of taking care of him and people feeling sorry for us, I don't have to do anything I don't want to do. This was the first time someone pushed me and built me up." Well, to know me is to know that no one ever cries alone in my presence. I started beaming and had streams of tears in my eyes. I could see her confidence build through this one simple experience, but what was amazing and brilliant is that as her confidence was growing so was mine. I felt like I was in the right job, in the right moment and with the right person. It was a feeling of confidence but more importantly one of contentment. My favorite feeling of all time.

There are just some things that don't fall into a perfect category of confidence. Being solar powered, being in my Jeep wrangler, accomplishing something really hard, and helping people find their own confidence don't fit into a magical checkbox, but I know in my heart that they all count.

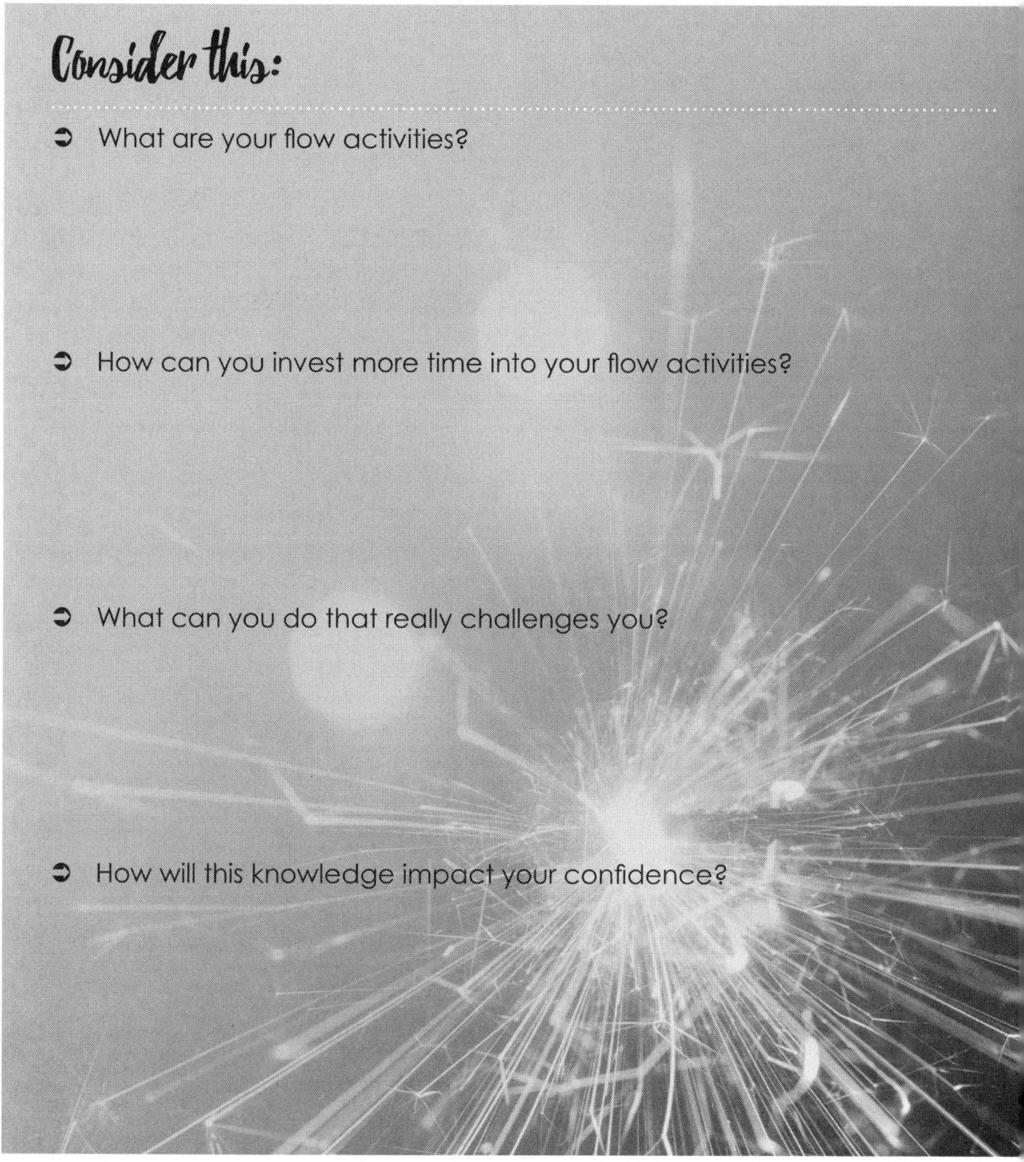

## Consider this:

- What are your flow activities?

- How can you invest more time into your flow activities?

- What can you do that really challenges you?

- How will this knowledge impact your confidence?

# 2.17

## NO UM, AH OR I'M SORRY

**I WAS ON A PHONE CALL FOR A COMMITTEE MEETING RECENTLY,** and as part of the first meeting, we shared our obligatory introductions with the team of volunteers. The first person on the agenda said, "Hi my name is James." Then, he stated all of his amazing involvements, his professional background, and noted his appreciation for this work group. What James did was very simple, but profound. As he was sharing, he spoke slowly and mindfully, but it was in sharp contrast to what happened next.

After 30 minutes of introductions, the lead coordinator began to speak. During his announcements and expectations, he stumbled and misspoke time and time again. I think it was part nerves, maybe even part exhaustion, but whatever it was, I could distinctly feel the difference between the ways these two men spoke. One was clearly confident, and the other was making me lose track of our tasks. The number of 'ums,' 'ahs,' and distracted pauses was out of hand, and it decreased his credibility quickly.

I am a huge fan of the work social psychologist Amy Cuddy does in the area of body language; and as a speaker, I am also fascinated by the delivery of language. The text, the context, the mood, the tone of voice, the pitch, and everything in between captivate me. After years of doing this work, I know my message can get lost resolutely when I add filler words to my stories. My bad habits include ums, ahs, and a horrible little sound of my lips smacking right before I start a sentence. Several years ago, my supervisor shared with me that when I am unsure of myself, I let the end of my sentences trail. I gave the excuse that I often have a hoarse voice due to my allergies, but in fact, it's true. When I am not feeling confident about my answer, the last three of four words mumble out of my mouth. Self-awareness is invaluable, but so is great feedback.

Yet even worse, I use the three highly popular words used by women across the globe: 'I'm sorry.'

This week, when I went to pick up my Yorkie at the dog hotel, (yes, they call it a hotel, yes, they even serve eggs, and yes he is spoiled) I was handed a can that was half full of his food. I stopped for a second, and confidently asked why I was getting his food back. The instructions were easy and clear - a half of a can the night before and the rest of the can in the morning. I was gone for 24 hours, but my suspicions led me to believe he missed a meal. Sadly, once my intuition was checked, it was confirmed they had forgotten a feeding. The guy running the boarding side of the business needed to say sorry, and he kindly did. I told him that mistakes happen, but that it was important to have a back up so it wouldn't occur again. (Here is where sorry counts.)

However, the woman in her car who was trying to get out of the parking lot at the same time as me didn't need to mouth, "I'm sorry," just because we were exiting at the same moment. The young man who took just an extra minute to help me get my bag down from the overhead bin didn't need to apologize either - he was helping me. The friend who ordered in line at Starbucks at the precise moment when I began my order didn't need to utter anything other than, "Go ahead - you first." Apologizing for nothing is out of control, and to be totally transparent, I had thought that only women were doing this, but I was wrong. We are all apologizing too much for ridiculous things.

For several years, I was in a Toastmasters club in town. One of the judges would share his feedback on our impromptu speeches, and every time I employed one of my bad habits, he would pound a penny on the table to remind me. It wasn't exactly kind, but it was trigger to mind the specifics. From my vantage point, all of my apologies, filler words, and mumbling sentences were leading people to the forgone conclusion that I am not confident. Whether consciously or unconsciously, the 'ums, 'ahs' and my horrible lip smacking must be picked up by others as a measure of how good I am at what I do, or how confident I am in my work. Since I get paid to speak – it all adds up.

Now, I am mindful of how I walk into a room, what I wear, and certainly how I shake someone's hand. I can't imagine writing a book about my own confidence without considering that all these subtle cues are connecting in other people's experiences with me, and they are judging whether or not I have it together. I use all of those cues when determining if someone is a good business contractor, an interesting client I want to serve, or if a new friend is worth my valuable time. So, I must consider the cues other people use to determine if I am right for them, too.

"I can't imagine writing a book about my own confidence without considering that all these subtle cues are connecting in other people's experiences with me, and they are judging whether or not I have it together."

I have moved these bad habits out of my blind spot and into my daily consciousness because I felt strongly that people read my level of confidence by my words, but more importantly by all the things I do and say in between those words. I am working on my posture, my pace and even my pregnant pauses, but I am really focusing in on the little details of how I deliver my confidence. Sorry, not sorry.

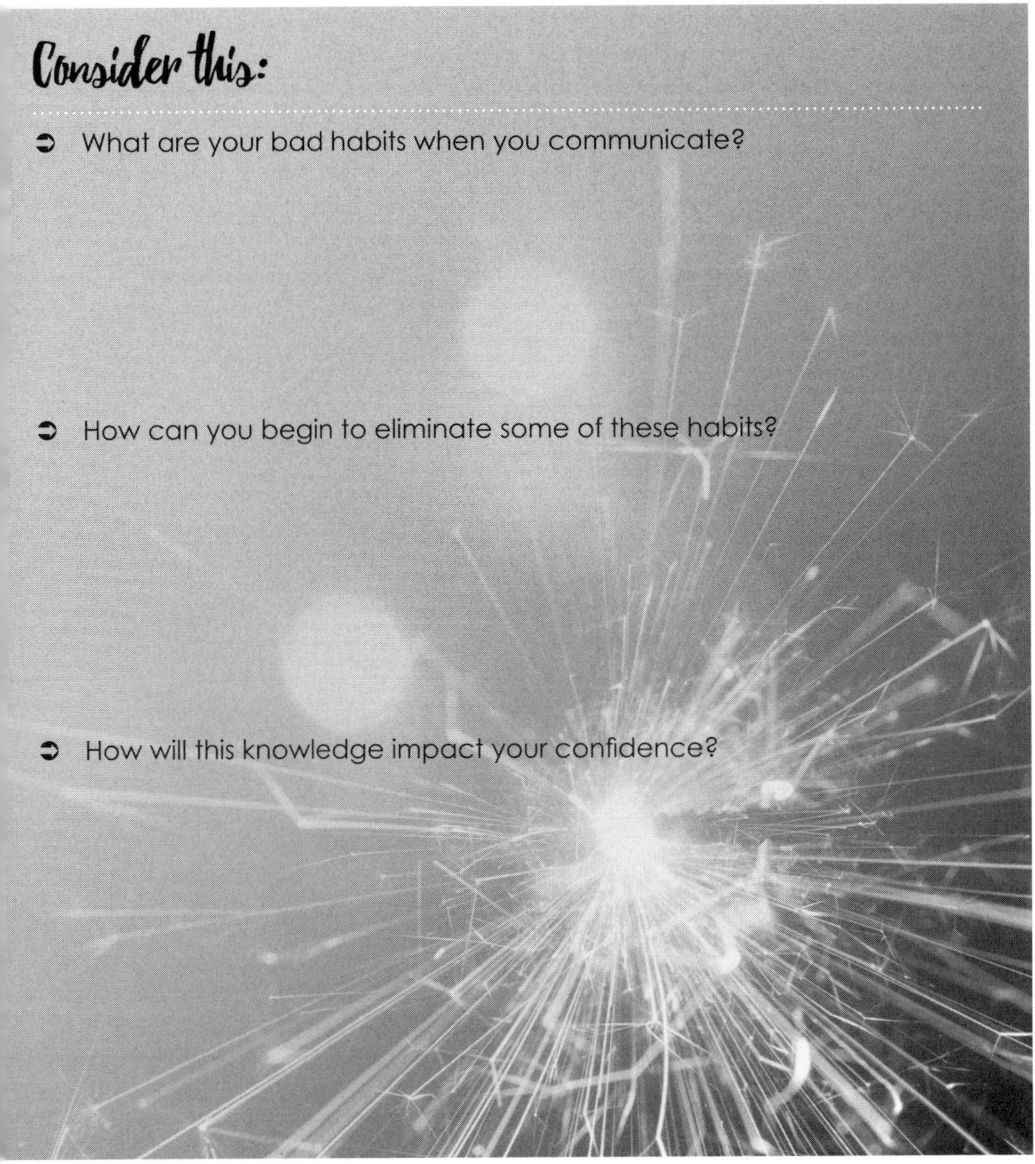

## Consider this:

- What are your bad habits when you communicate?

- How can you begin to eliminate some of these habits?

- How will this knowledge impact your confidence?

# 2.18

## PRACTICAL SHOES, ERIN

**RECENTLY, I HAD 14 NEIGHBORS OVER FOR A NIGHT OF CONNECTION, AND LET'S BE HONEST, A LITTLE WINE.** I was inspired to get these incredible women together for a few months, not because I love to cook or even clean up after a long night, but I know that in the middle of the Midwest in the winter, it's cold and dreary, and in some way bringing loud and funny women together makes it not so cold and dreary. Plus, my sweet friend Ellen reminded me of a universal truth. We need each other.

When Ellen and her husband were moving into their new house, the old owners threw a party. Instead of having a going away party for themselves, they did something remarkably kind. They invited Ellen and her family over so that they could meet all of their new neighbors. It got to me in a way that was a bit unexpected. It was a reminder that it would have been so easy for them to want to complain over the price they got, or what repairs Ellen wanted done before closing, but instead, they chose graciousness above anything else. They helped Ellen build her new community as they were leaving theirs.

In the past few months, we have had at least five new families move to our neighborhood, and one curmudgeon who refuses to find another place despite how miserable he makes everyone. So, in the spirit, I decided to offer up my house so 14 beautiful women had a chance to connect.

That night reminded me that women crave real connection. They shared more than things like what you can find at their house if you forget something at the grocery store. Not to anyone's surprise, sugar and wine were at the top of the list. We talked about new love, painful divorces, which contractor to use when your furnace goes out and everything in between. Even the new women who only knew me started talking about real stuff. Then, the next day, the texts started flying. There were texts of gratefulness, but also joy about being connected to so many amazing human beings. Really simple things in life are what matter most.

I've been thinking a lot about joy, grace, gratitude, and real life connections and the link to confidence a lot lately. This month marks five years since I went to Colorado to visit my friend Mary Ann and spend some quality time with her son – who was living with a relentless diagnosis of cancer. I knew at the time that he was terminally ill, and at five years old, it was, with certainty, going to be his last trip around the sun.

Mary Ann and her husband had set up a year of living for him - a trip to Disney with his sister, and massive amounts of time on putt-putt courses. When I was there for a weekend visit, we went into Denver to see the *Lion King* and went out for dinner at Red Robin – where, if memory serves me correctly, the fries are endless. Then, during my last afternoon, we made snow angels. The irony was not lost of me in the moment. It took us hours to put on massive amounts of snow gear, but we ended up taking family photos, swinging at the playground and then lying in the snow while the sun warmed us. We took pictures to capture the current joy – things we now look on to remember his life and to mark his time.

A few months later, when I got the call that her sweet boy had passed away at home, I didn't cry. I was unbelievably sad, but for all the tears I have shed in my life, I didn't cry. I did what Mary Ann would want me to do - I called my parents, and we booked tickets to join her in honoring her son.

The night that I got into their small town in Colorado, my mom and dad told me to take the rental to go see her right away. When I walked into the house, there was my friend – the one who taught me how to pee in the woods without getting stung on the rear end, how to cook a beautiful meal over an open fire, and how to be the world's best MC at opening and closing sessions of camp. But now, she was a mother without a child – not my once 19 year old friend who was conspiring with me to go see her Australian boyfriend who was stuck in Canada.

When I opened the door, I saw her as she sat in her kitchen and smiled. She was heartbroken, but instead of being miserable, she chose to be in the moment. She looked over at me and said, "Now listen. I told you to bring the right shoes when you carry his casket up the side of the mountain. It's rocky and if you think you are going to be cute tomorrow, you are crazy." There she was in the midst of tragedy reminding me to be practical. I wanted to hug her, and then I realized, selfishly, I just wanted her to console me. Instead what she taught me was to pull myself together, to wear appropriate shoes, and for God's sake not to make a fool of myself as a pallbearer.

The next day, I walked in the church and saw her standing at the entrance greeting guests, but this time she was in a linen dress that was black. A black dress her sister made her to signify that she was the mother of a son who passed away, and I lost it. I completely unraveled, and disappeared into a hall closet and started bawling. My dad found me and asked if I needed a minute, but I needed more than a minute; I was in the middle of a cry where you can barely breathe.

To be certain, the universe was watching the whole thing from a distance, and of course, Mary Ann found me. She smiled, cried with me for a moment, and then told me to pull it together. She wanted this to be a celebration, and for all the years I have known her, I felt like she wanted us to have joy - joy that he lived, that he was hers, and despite the fact that he passed, we were there to honor him.

I sat in a row with just two big, stoic men. One was her sweet brother and the other a cousin. We all cried – holding hands and wiping noses. There was not enough Kleenex in the entire state of Colorado to handle all of the sadness, but then something happened.

We left for the mountainside burial, and I walked up the side of the foothill grave with five other men – also in Mary Ann's approved list of practical shoes. I let my hand touch the beautiful casket before it was lowered into the ground, and then I heard dozens of people start singing. I looked down, and there were dozens of voices singing Riley's favorite camp song. To this day, I have no memory of what song they picked, but I know that it was overwhelmingly joyful to be in the presence of sadness and veracity at the same exact moment.

My take-a-way is that it all counts. All of the connections, the relationships, the heartaches, the surrendered joy, and the graciousness add up. I have no idea what is really going to happen next, but I do know that I wouldn't want to miss out on any of it. I don't want to be the woman that sits in the hole, too scared to live – even if it means that next to confidence and joy, I will have to endure heartache. I want to be the woman who boldly chooses it all – confidently. I don't wish what Mary Ann had to go through on anyone, but what I was reminded was that even though Mary Ann didn't choose this, she did choose how she handled it, how she let it be a part of her narrative, but not own her, and how she taught everyone else around her to do the same. To live confidently.

"My take-a-way is that it all counts. All of the connections, relationships, the heartaches, the surrendered joy, and the graciousness add up."

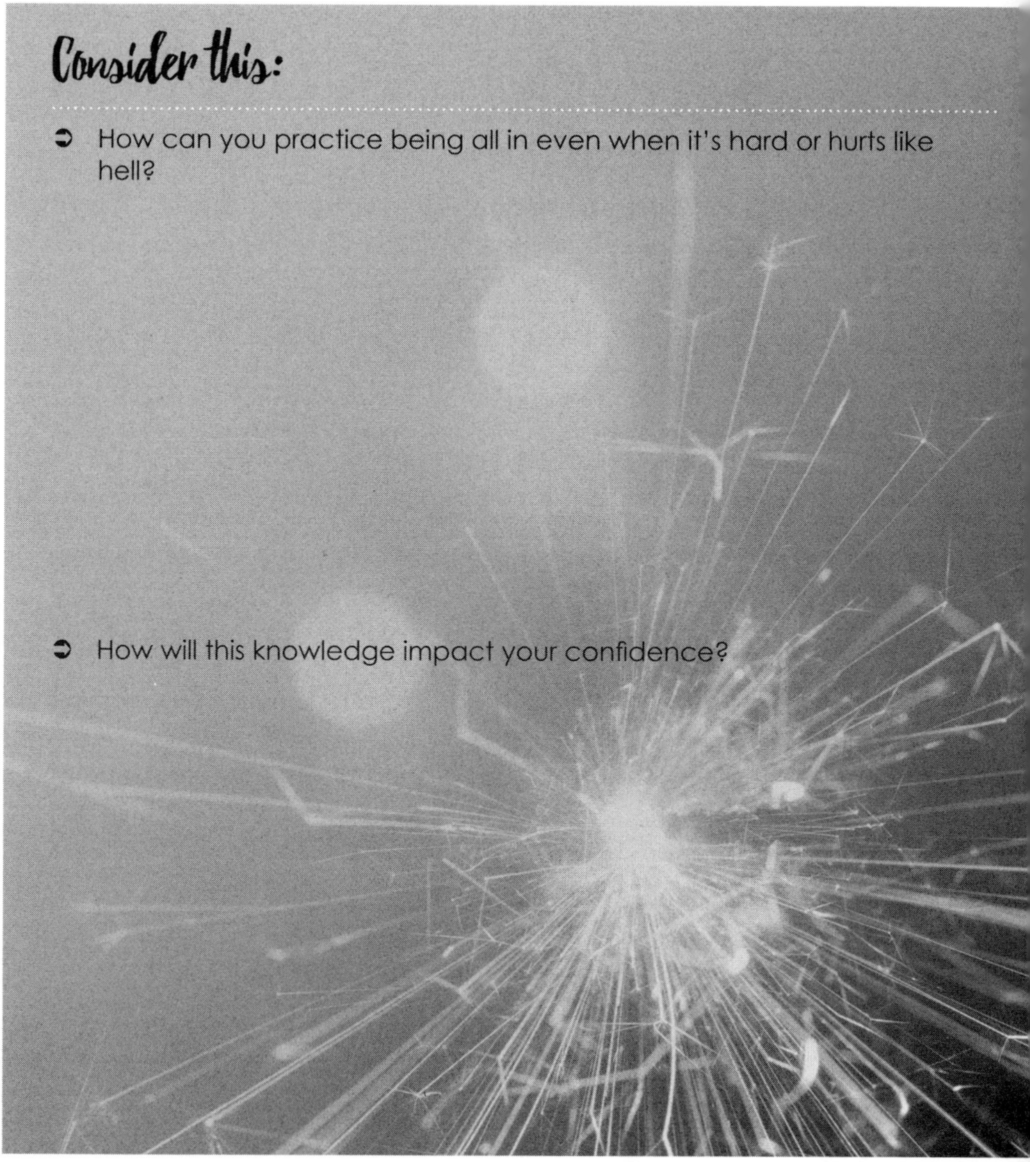

## Consider this:

- How can you practice being all in even when it's hard or hurts like hell?

- How will this knowledge impact your confidence?

# what i learned along the way

# 2.19

DON'T BLOCK THE BLESSING

**A FEW YEARS AGO, I HEARD A REVEREND SHARE A MESSAGE CALLED *DON'T BLOCK THE BLESSING*.** It was as if this man was inside my head – and in some way could pinpoint something that, at the time, I couldn't even name or describe - but knew to be true. He said, "Don't be afraid when things are at their best."

His premise was simple. He shared that when so many of us start to run on all cylinders, we instantly think, "No one can be this happy, it's all going to go to drop at any moment." He started talking about how we sabotage our happiness (and confidence) when too many things are looking up for us. Then, he said something even smarter. He doubled down on his message and whispered, "When things are going really well, ask for more." What?!?! "Look for it." he said.

I used to believe in balance, and had this horrible notion that everything sat in a state of yin and yang, which meant that if one part of my life was exceptional, something else was bound to be out of place. So, if we had a glorious summer, we were bound for a miserable winter. If we had a really good financial year or a promotion, things would even out the next year and the universe would prove its need to be in equilibrium (like a roof leak or a car breaking down). If all of my family members were getting along, someone was bound to feel disappointed or displeased soon. Continual or consistent joy - that would be just too much.

I had this mantra revolving around my conception of living a life of balance, but my thinking was in a weird rut. My head said that happiness was paired with unhappiness. They didn't show up at the same time, but they were like two little kids always vying for attention. Then, I came to the realization that I have so little control in this world. I mean, I have control over what comes out of my mouth, but in the vastness of possibility, I have so little force over what really happens each day. So, I started taking stock. I have control over me, my work, my relationships, my kindness (or unkindness when I am hangry) and well, that's about it. Instead of trying to anticipate bad things, I want to start reveling in the good stuff and expecting that more joy is right around the corner – even if it might not be. All of this for the simple fact that if I don't, I am missing out of being present.

Then, I realized I was doing this for protection. When I am not surprised by bad news, or when I am already in the state of anticipation, the bad times won't hurt so badly. But, it's BS. I can't temper my every moment of confidence with the sinking feeling of what is lurking.

Then, during the funeral of my son's friend, I realized that no matter what I ask from the universe, bad things might still happen. Tempering my luck, my fortune or my excitement level is not going to stop someone from getting cancer. Being overly cautious and concerned was not going to prevent heartache later. What I was doing was mitigating true happiness. I thought that if I didn't revel in the most amazing things coming into my life that in some way, I could hold back the potential bad stuff. As I write about this, it sounds ridiculous on paper. But in fairness, I don't think I am alone. So many of my closest friends feel the same way.

When I ask my friend Ashley how she is doing. She always says, "Well, I'm great today, but you know something bad is right around the corner." It is as if we were taught to be so humble or conversely so scared of joy that we can't let it all of the goodness seep in.

This. This messes with my confidence. Now, I am in the practice of being humble, and humbleness is probably one of my top values, but what I have started to see is that being humble is different than being confident.

Furthermore, I let go of being perfect, and I am in the practice of being a One Trick Pony. I have made a decision to figure out what I do really well and spend my time killing it in this area.

I just got back from a huge conference, and was met with a dozen emails of thanks from people who sat in my three breakout sessions. Getting compliments is so hard for me, and even when someone told me my session was life changing I had to remind myself to take it all in with appreciation. These words of affirmation don't signify in anyway a spiral of madness that is about to ring at my door. Well, maybe they do, but what is the point of blocking the blessing of appreciation from someone – just in case.

So, my mindset began to change. Instead of looking for all the bad things going on and guaranteeing myself that something great is right around the corner, or looking for all the great things and thinking the shoe is going to drop, I take each experience as it comes. I am practicing spending less time worrying what is happening next and a bit more time worrying about what is happening now. It's called living in the moment.

"I am practicing spending less time worrying about what is happening next and a bit more time worrying about what is happing now. It's called living in the moment."

I will still be uber organized, always have a strategy, and require flexibility through all of it, but I don't want to miss out on the high. I want to be in the practice of being like a little kid who lights up when they get the one present they didn't think they would get. I want to be like the Grandma in the viral video who dances and cries when she finds out her daughter is pregnant. I want to be like the Cubs who won the World Series - always optimistic, even when losing, and celebrating like mad when the win finally arrives.

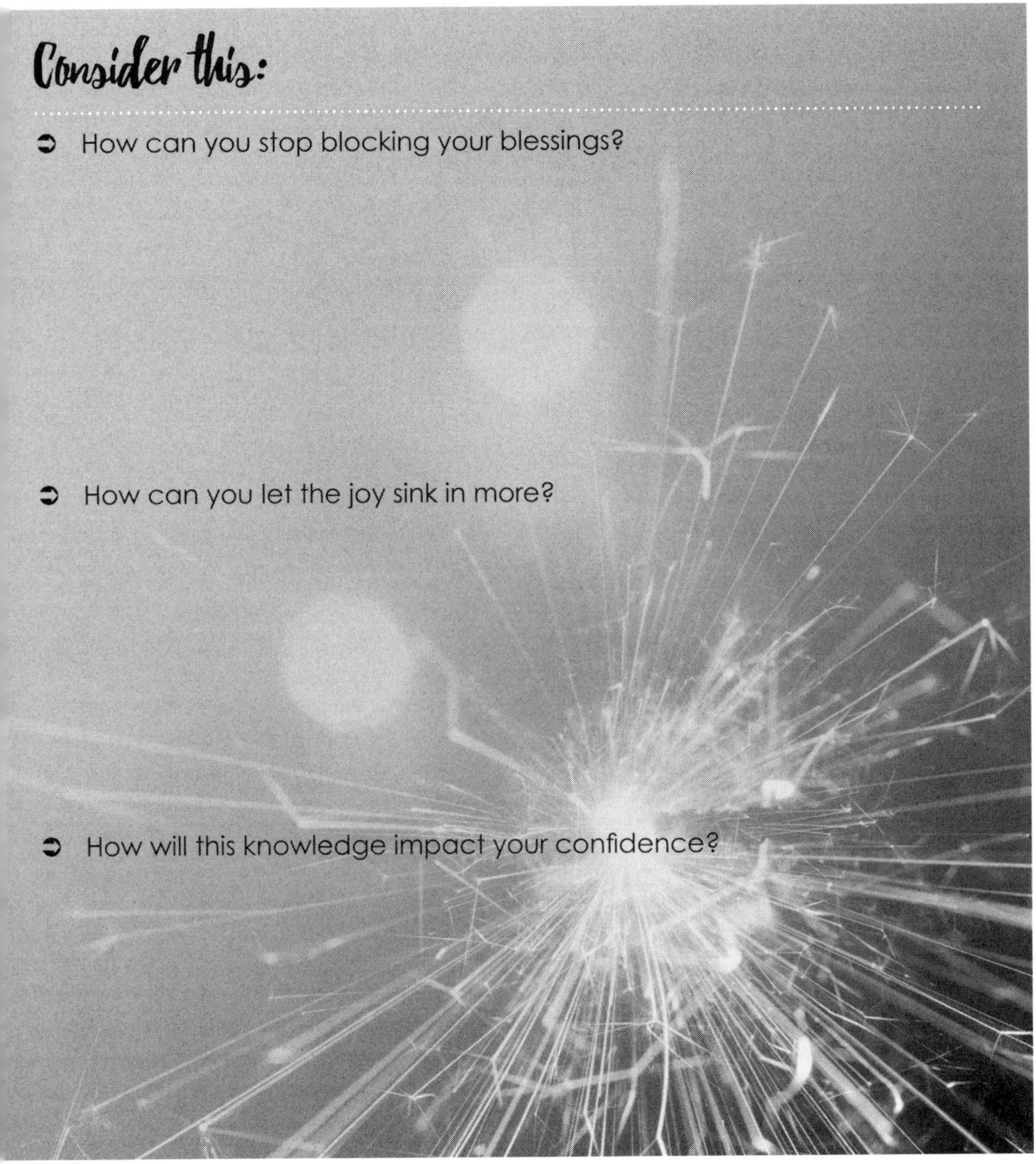

## Consider this:

- How can you stop blocking your blessings?
- How can you let the joy sink in more?
- How will this knowledge impact your confidence?

# what i learned along the way

# 2.20

## I GOT SHOULDED ON

**ON MOST DAYS, MY CUP IS SO FULL THAT IT IS OVERFLOWING.** This last work trip was a huge reminder of that, and yet there are reminders all around me to keep confidence at the forefront of my mind. I have said it before, but I am in the practice of being consciously confident, and here I sit with another fabulous lesson.

I was minutes away from being "shoulded upon" yet I sat completely unaware as to what was about to happen in my brain. It was the third trip to California in the past few months. This time, I just finished two sessions at a national conference in Long Beach, California. It's really hard for me to say no to California.

I arrived in this seemingly quiet town right before the holidays, and I was totally shocked that two of my favorite clients, who have turned into friends, were attending the same event. Now, I am smart enough to know that, as an introvert, I can't ever stay at the conference hotel. I hate the shaming looks as well as the awkward chit-chat in the elevators. (Yes, I do want to sneak away from all humans while a big session is going on, and please, no, don't look at me like that!) But, over the course of two and a half days, I ran into another colleague who did a huge service immersion trip to New Orleans with me, and we reminisced about how kick-ass that week of service was. Then, I ran into Krystal, a woman who speaks for me in the summers, and I was reminded that she is simply incredible. Finally, one night I got to have a short, but fabulous dinner with my two friends, Jen and Alexis.

> "Yes, I do want to sneak away from all humans while a big session is going on, and please, no, don't look at me like that!"

After all of these amazing connections, I ended up running two sessions with out-of-this-world feedback, and had dinner with one of my favorite families: The Greenbergs (not the TV show family, but the actual Greenberg family whom I have loved for years).

Then, it happened. I returned my rental car after the conference and got on the big bus back to LAX. I sat and stared at a family who was talking to their three year old about why they were flying that day as he bounced on his seat standing up. They leaned over with excitement and told him they were going to Hawaii. (Insert jealousy here.) He kept talking about how he only wanted to go for a day and a night because he really wanted to stay back at his grandma and grandpa's place. They reminded him that there is a lot of fun happening in Hawaii, including swimming, and he kindly kept talking about his grandma and grandpa. The entire thing was adorable.

I realized that I needed to pull my wallet so I could get a tip for the driver. I looked in my bag and only had a $20 bill. It's rare that I carry cash, so this is a miracle into itself, but then I started to over think the entire situation. Should I give the driver this $20 tip, even though he only moved one small bag for me? Should I give the driver a $20 tip, since I know that most people are bad tippers? Should I give the driver a $20 tip since it is the holidays and everyone can use an extra buck? Should I just grab my bag and run before he even sees me get off the bus?

I got "shoulded" on. The pressure of what I "should" do was speeding through my mind instead of simply enjoying this little passenger talk about planes, Hawaii, and grandma and grandpa.

What I know to be true is that there are a lot of expectations placed on women. Be cute, be nice, be smart, but don't ever brag about how cute, nice and smart you are. Be giving, be forgiving, find the joy in life, and be certain not to complain, because you are lucky. It's true, I am lucky, but to be honest, I give up a lot of what I want to fill other people's expectation, and as a result, I am "shoulded" on way more than I want. Because I want you to think I have it all together, or because I admire other women who seem to have it all together, I put a lot of pressure on myself to follow certain rules.

So, you know what I did? I realized what was happening in my brain, and after a few prolonged minutes, I decided that I didn't have to tip him – at all. I didn't have to avoid him, or run off the bus, but instead, I leaned over made some great conversation with him, told him I would be grabbing my own bag, and wished him very happy holidays. That was it, and again, no one died. I gave myself simultaneous permission to not tip him, but not to avoid him either. He is in a tough customer service job with little praise or appreciation. So, my tip was to be a human being and have a real conversation – and learn the lesson. Avoid getting shoulded on.

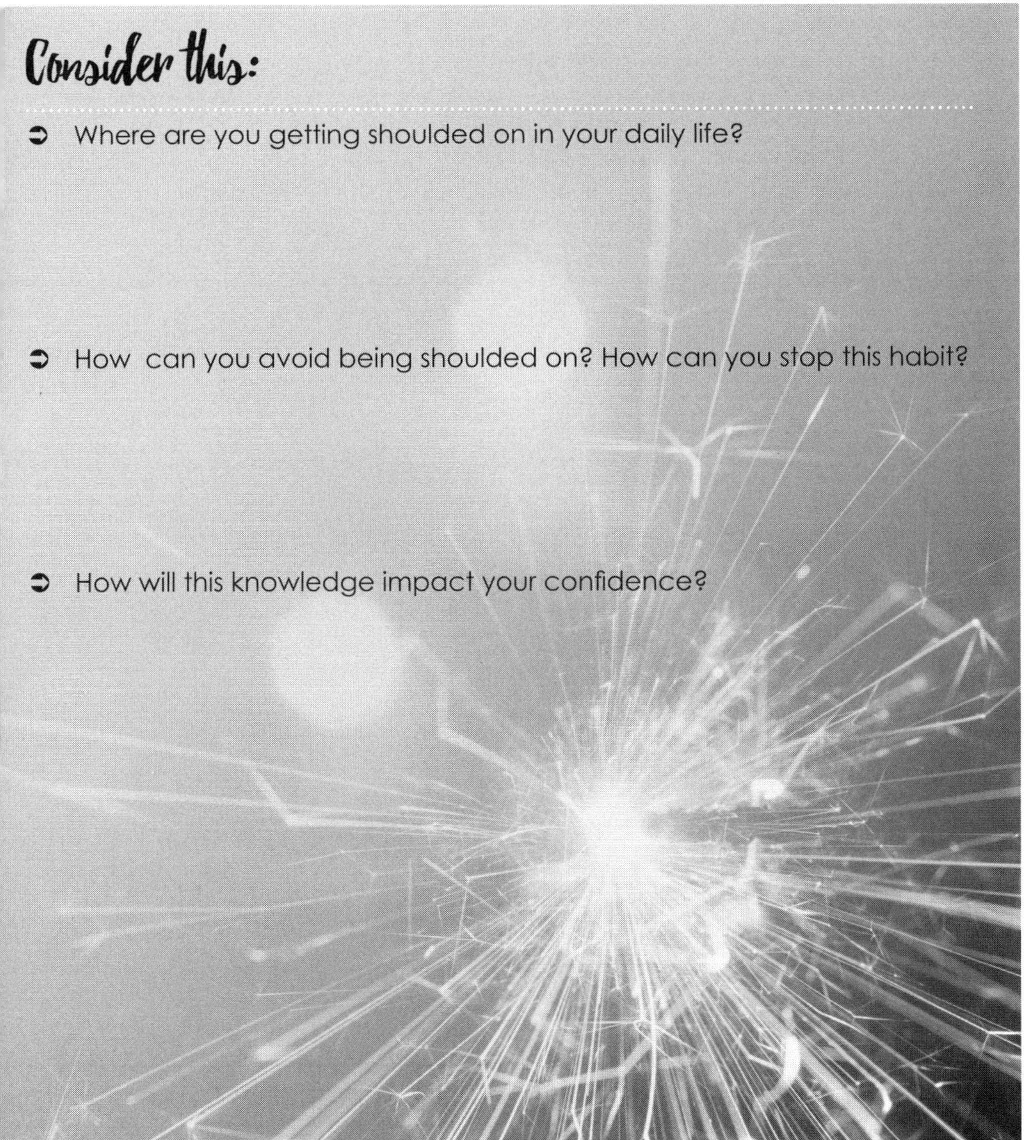

## Consider this:

- Where are you getting shoulded on in your daily life?

- How  can you avoid being shoulded on? How can you stop this habit?

- How will this knowledge impact your confidence?

what i learned along the way

# 2.21

## WHAT? NO MASTER PLAN?

**ABOUT FIVE YEARS AGO,** I was asked to meet with a gentleman who was in charge of a division of a large company that sold residential security systems. It was not exactly my forte – to say the least, but one of my colleagues Amanda wanted me to meet him. He too had started his own company, and then got the pull to come back to the corporate life working for an organization that believed in a single priority: To develop humans, first. The product could have been anything, he said, but the reason for their existence was to support the growth of the employees through personal development. Sales guys and home installers were getting trained in their jobs and in life. It was fascinating. In my idealistic world, I thought it was so cool that a company really committed to humans. There are a lot of companies who say they value people, but I know that they do only when said humans perform, make numbers, or create something new that will keep the company afloat. This company was committing in a way that I had never seen.

I was asked to bring in my resume, even though it was not an interview. I sat down with this gentleman, and he immediately started asking interview questions. I was mad. I like to prepare, but then I realized, sometimes you just need to be in the moment and not over think every possible question like, "So tell me about yourself."

We talked about my work in non-profits, including being a camp director, how I loved to travel, how I was pretty keen on writing leadership curriculum, and even how we root for our basketball team. We weaved in and out of so many topics that morning, but the one thing I remember is that this guy was also a big believer in servant leadership – the style of leadership that focuses on a question that author and philosopher Robert Greenleaf asks. Greenleaf remind us, "The best test, and difficult to administer, is: Do those served grow as persons? Do they, while being served, become healthier, wiser, freer, more autonomous, more likely themselves to become servants?" The leadership nerd in me was delighted. How do we serve others? That is the real question.

As we were finishing up our non-interview interview, I was asked the closer. You know - the question that can make or break you. Here it was, hanging in the room for me. "So, what are your five-year and ten-year goals?" I had built rapport, made him laugh, dropped in servant leadership, and even talked about sports for crying out loud. But since I had not prepared a thing, I took a huge risk and answered honestly. "I don't have any long term plans. To be honest, I have found that I could have never dreamed of any of this. I could not have guessed I would be doing the things that I actually love doing at this age, and on top of it, I have seen so much of the world that I never expected to see. So, I have a vision board that is laminated, but other than that, I don't have a plan to have a plan."

He listened, and I waited for his judgmental response, but on that day there was not a one. Instead he said, "Finally, an interesting answer from someone sitting in that chair." He went on to say that he, too, did not have a master plan or a full life strategy. Then, I opened up a bit more and told him I thought it was a waste of time. My goal is to press on, while simultaneously being really open to the next adventure. I can imagine how hard it is to get an opportunity that is incredible and having to turn it down because it's not on my schematic. I want the freedom to be able to pursue what is important, what lines up with my values, and what will help me grow, not something that will help me climb some imaginary corporate ladder. I have a set of filters for sure, and a vision of what I want, but there is no color-coded document.

So, I walked out, got asked to meet with a second person days later, and eventually walked back in completely unaware of what was happening. I was being asked to interview for a role in developing sales training – which at the time, I had no desire or, more importantly knowledge in. The kind woman kept telling me, "We hire for the right fit, and we can teach you everything else." Plan or no plan, I was not ready to be in charge of a massive company's sales strategy in the training department. So I quietly, but confidently told her, after just about 10 minutes, that I was not the right candidate. I walked out with my head high while I did something that was really hard that day and most days. Saying no.

Then, as my 40th birthday arrived this year, I kept getting calls from young professionals in my industry. They wanted to sit down to talk about my company and the work that I do, but I realized pretty quickly it was a guise. They were coming to me to tell me that they were scared, bored, confused, lost, and unhappy. They all had great jobs and great supervisors, but they felt like something big was missing. When I finally figured out was going on, I shared one bit of wisdom that was shared with me.

**Your 20s are all about discovery. It's a chance to listen and learn, and get your hands dirty. Don't worry about your job title, worry about the exploration of your roles. Volunteer, say yes, stay late, but don't feel the pressure to have it all figured out yet.**

**Your 30s are about narrowing your scope while trying to uncover the pattern of things you love to do. Observe your best boss and your worst boss, and take a lot of notes. Find what tasks bring your energy and which ones suck the life out of you.**

**Your 40s are about realizing you can't be a Jack or Jill of all trades, so find the work that makes your happy. Go back and mark the pattern, find the highlights and start making your way toward a place that you can make a difference.**

**Your 50s and 60s are all about giving back while finally making some real money. Invest in relationships, build up other people, mentor, sponsor, and make sure that you are still getting energy out of the things that once brought you so much. If not, it's time to reinvent, again.**

These five women who kept asking me to lunch were trying to get to their

60s before they even made it through their 20s. Unknowingly, they wanted to skip their "get your hands dirty" part and go straight to the "I have arrived and can breathe" part. When I talked to them about this process, I could see that they started to relax – a lot.

Then, I had an 'aha' moment. One of the women, whom I adore, was talking to me about her years as a professional dancer. She shared how much she loves her current work, but how something didn't feel right. She couldn't pinpoint it, name it, or place a label on it, but she knew in her gut something just wasn't right. After two rounds of coffee, I leaned over and said, "Can I ask you a question? You loved being a dancer more than anything else, despite the fact there was no money and your body constantly hurt. Are you looking for that same feeling again?" She sweetly smiled and said, "Yes. That's it. Even though it was so painful, I loved every minute of it. It was my vision since I was ten years old, and now that it is gone, I am worried that I won't ever get that feeling back."

I wanted to cry for her. How amazing it is to know your purpose so early on in life, and in the same breath, I also thought, how sad it must be for her to think she can never get it back. But, I am smarter with age, and I shared back, "Start dreaming again. Get out your magazines, your scissors and your glue, and put a vision board together over break. Let's figure out the next amazing thing that is going to happen to you."

What I have realized, is that no matter what age I am, I will always be looking for that spark, that one thing that makes me feel really alive. Hence the cover of this book. Now, I have two plans. First, I still am working on not having a master plan, and second; I should always be on the lookout for the work that gives me feel that unmistakable feeing. It's part of having a purpose, part using my talents, part doing good or giving back, part excelling at something, and part feeling like my body is on fire from all of the hard work I put into it.

## Consider this:

- What creates a spark in you or makes your feel alive?

- What is your vision, your focus, or your filters - instead of your master plan?

- How will this knowledge work to impact your confidence?

# Section Three:
# What I Know Now

# what i know now

# 3.1

## PERMISSION TO BE RADICALLY UNFINISHED

**OVER THE PAST TWO AND A HALF YEARS, I HAVE FOUND THAT PEOPLE POST ABOUT ME OR SAY THINGS LIKE, "I HAVE HEARD ABOUT YOU BEFORE, AND YOU ARE REALLY AMAZING."** It is a combination of sweetness and total embarrassment. I literally feel those two things instantly and concurrently. I have never wanted to be the center of attention – ever. But, I remember standing outside of a college this fall in Boston and having seven students who hired me walk me to my Uber. They shyly said to me, "Can we get a picture with you? We are huge fans, and what you did tonight on stage was unreal." In that moment, I wanted to say to them: When I get back to the hotel, I have to eat a sandwich, just like you do, I have to do homework, just like you do, I have to pee and brush my teeth, watch CNN, and get an early wake up call, just like you do. I am totally normal and average. My job is just different than yours, so don't ever feel like I am on a pedestal.

One of the biggest conclusions I have arrived at from this projects is that I am as normal as they come, and I am starting to realize what a gift it is to be completely and utterly average. What I know to be true is that I am striving for a life full of confident living, but I am clearly, precisely and happily not striving for exceptionality. Rarity, extraordinariness, uniqueness or remarkability are no longer my target. As a matter of fact, I am inclined to live in this state of incompleteness. I am giving myself permission to be radically unfinished.

> "As a matter of fact, I am inclined to live in this state of incompleteness. I am giving myself permission to be radically unfinished."

Now, I annoy the crap out of my husband when I leave stacks of paper on every surface, drop clean clothes (sorted) in the hallway for days, or even walk by the piles of things that need to go up the stairs, but this space of incompleteness is different.

Right now, being radically unfinished means that I am giving myself full permission to make bigger and bolder mistakes, and to stop trying to prove to everyone that I have arrived. Furthermore, I am making a new commitment to stop comparing. I am exceptional at feeling less due to my perceived notion of what someone else has in their life that seems to be farther along than what I have going on in mine.

I have moved too many friends into bigger houses, been picked up to go to dinner in fancier cars, and even been graced with someone who got a huge promotion and wants to pick up the check at the end of a meal. I have felt my heart twinge with a bit of jealousy and a hell of a lot of comparison. It is utterly and completely ridiculous because this comparison is on the map pointed toward exceptionality – a plan that is just too exhausting for me.

One of my friends, Brendon, and I talk about how the world is full of abundance in ways we don't consider. This world lacks so much, yet in the areas where we can make the biggest strides, we should never compete. There will never be enough people talking about confidence for women, there will never be enough people focusing on the development of children, there will never be enough fundraising to save animals, or to create technology that stops children from dying from cancer. So instead of living a life with a deficit mindset, I am going to practice giving instead of counting.

It's easy to count other people's number of friends on social media, their likes on Instagram, the number of parties they got invited to, the number of vacations they take, and so on and so on and so on. I have realized that the counting will never end, so I am trying not to arrive. I am trying to work – at being unfinished. It's such a freeing thing for me because it allows me to still create and be creative. Two things I revel in.

I am starting to lean back into a private thought of mine that is simple: I am a late bloomer. I always have been and I always will be. I am on my own timeline, partly due to my own stubbornness, but partly due to the fact that I am an observer, first. I dream big, and then calculate how it will all unfold. This. This part takes time, which means that I am leaning into my new thought of being radically unfinished.

I have realized that I am doing all of this for two reasons. First, I want to grow. Second, my interrupted, messy, not-so-perfect path will force other women to examine how happy and confident they can be while being in the place of uncertainty. Not one damn person has it all figured out, and if I can share that piece of wisdom with other women, it is a win for all of us.

Have the courage to be confident and radically unfinished.

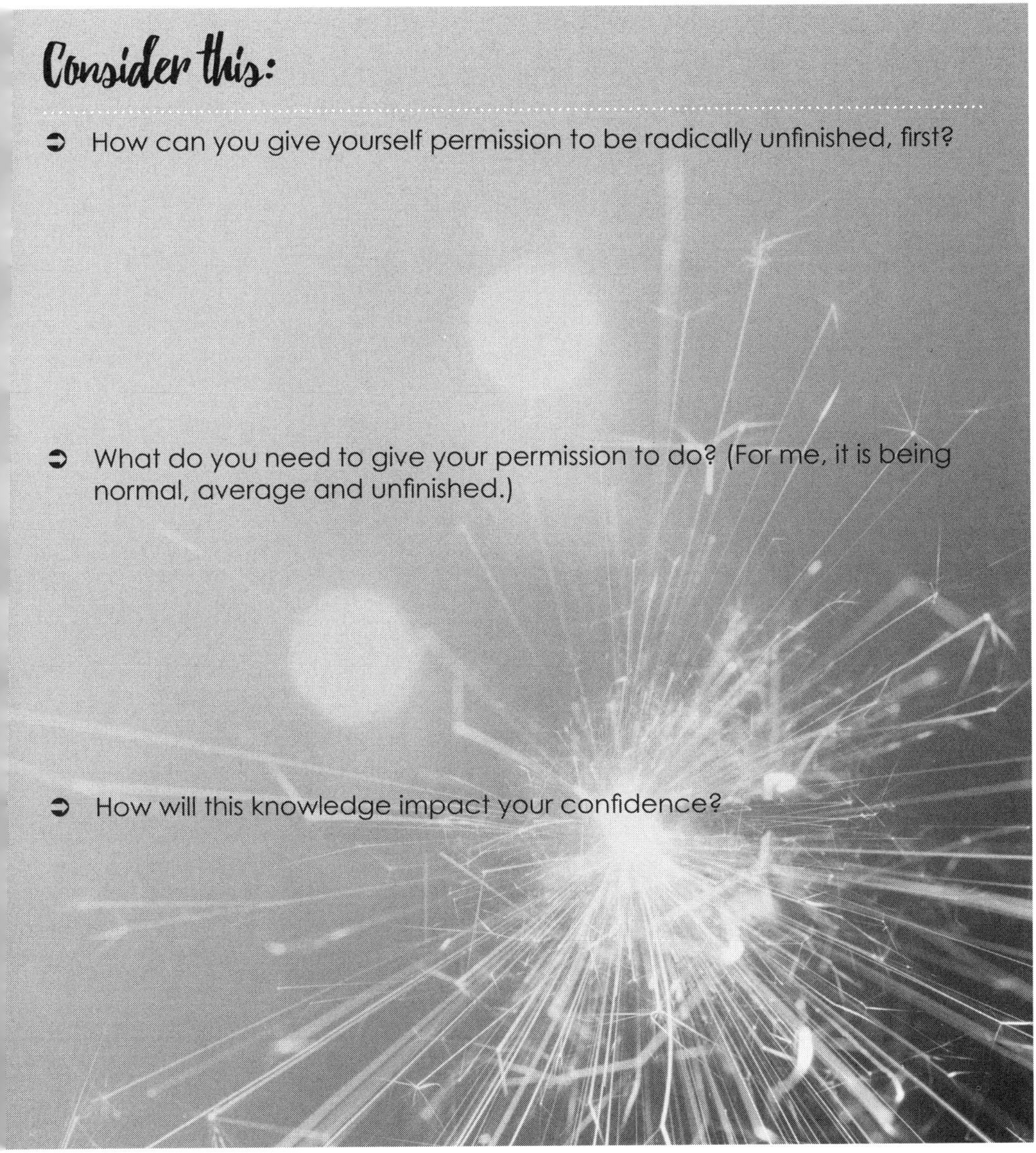

## Consider this:

- How can you give yourself permission to be radically unfinished, first?

- What do you need to give your permission to do? (For me, it is being normal, average and unfinished.)

- How will this knowledge impact your confidence?

# what i know now

# 3.2

MY BIGGEST TAKE-A-WAYS

Collecting the Wisdom

1. **PEOPLE MATTER TO MY CONFIDENCE.** My dad is my biggest cheerleader, and my mom is my greatest encourager. Without them, I would not be as bold and confident as I am today. The wrong people in my life, however, can do damage, so I am much more mindful of my relationships today than I have ever been.
2. In return, people need me. For a long time, I assumed that I didn't have anything special or magical to share, but at this stage in my life, I have done just enough living that I have real wisdom. More importantly, I know that is not just about wisdom sharing, it is about listening. In order to help other women, I am NOT waiting to arrive, because it will never happen.
3. When I owned and exposed my fears, they started to fade quickly. I wish I had done this activity a million years ago. It started out scary and ended up being so cathartic and liberating.
4. When I took a relentless inventory of myself, I realized that I am complex, but will never make excuses for how detailed and intricate I am. I don't blame other people who don't understand me right away, but I am not trying to fit into someone else's checkbox.
5. I have to get out of my head.

6. Defining authentic confidence is hard, but so worthwhile. It's slippery and confusing. There is no definitive path on how to get there, but nearly every woman I have shared this project with has said, "When will that book be done? I need to read it now." This is a reminder to me to talk about the tough stuff.
7. I am really comfortable not being all things to all people, FINALLY. I am magical in a few small areas, and I am done trying to be everything, or worse, trying to be perfect.
8. I must practice confidence. Every. Single. Day. It is like eating healthy and exercising. I am making a lifelong commitment.

"I must practice confidence. Every. Single. Day.
It is like eating healthy and exercising.
I am making a lifelong commitment."

9. I live by a great quote from Albert F. Schlieder that reads, "We tend to judge others by their behavior and ourselves by our intentions." It is a reminder for me to be kinder to people when I want to judge. We are great at being the only exception to the rule when in fact everyone takes turns driving the struggle bus. Grace is key.
10. I have to get out of my head!
11. I want to silence the stuff that gets in the way of my joy or real connections in life. I don't want to block all the blessings. I want to expect more joy, happiness, and authentic confidence to come my way.
12. I believe in the 10,000 hour rule when it comes to confidence. The author Malcolm Gladwell wrote, "...ten thousand hours is the magic number of greatness." It's likely that it will take most of us at least that amount of time to get to authentic confidence. So, it's time for us to put our seat belts on.

13. People don't notice internal changes like they do an external change (bad haircut, anyone?) So, I can't worry too much if not everyone sees how much stronger I am inside right away. I am settled in knowing it's invaluable work regardless.
14. Oh! Wearing great underwear is a huge key to confidence. There is nothing worse than walking on stage with a wedgie. Cute or practical? Either way is fine – just as long as I don't look like a fool trying to adjust my underwear in front a  thousand people. The details add up.
15. I have to get out of my head ;)
16. Being a people pleaser is physically draining and exhausting. I am over being a people pleaser for my own health. I am ready to say no a lot more.
17. Being radically unfinished is like getting a permanent permission slip to be authentically human.
18. Sometimes, when I am not feeling confident, I try and give it to others. There is a magic power in this practice, and it seems confidence always comes back to me.
19. Authentic confidence is attractive. This summer, I ran from an event hotel near the Atlanta airport to catch a flight to another city. I had just finished delivering a phenomenal keynote to 1,300 people, and I was on cloud nine. I sat down to charge my phone at the gate, and I caught a gentleman staring at me. After a few awkward minutes, he leaned over and said, "You are probably the most beautiful women I have ever met."  What I wanted to say to him is, "That's not true at all. What you see is that, right now, in this moment, I am the most happy and authentically confident women you have ever met, and that my friend is worth way more than beauty."  Confidence can come and go, but I think people can read it on our bodies when we are radiating with it  - and it's highly attractive.
20. I am getting out of my head . . .

There is one more thing I learned from being an author that I want to own. I am terrified of people finding grammar mistakes in my work. It is a huge trigger for me, but as I shared with a young man who bought my last book and wanted a refund after finding mistakes: I don't write to win grammar awards, I write to share my stories in order to serve other people.

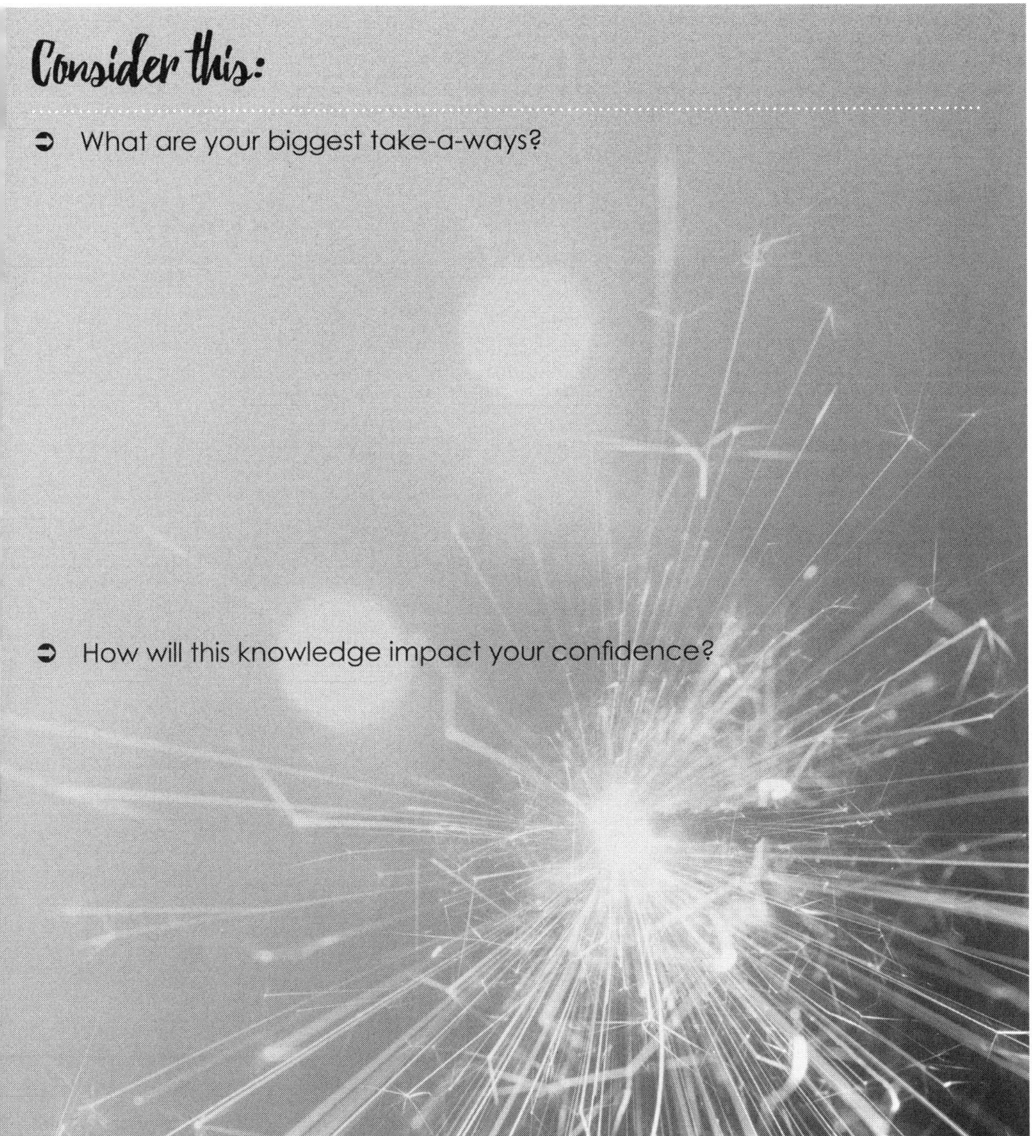

## Consider this:

- What are your biggest take-a-ways?

- How will this knowledge impact your confidence?

# references

Chapman, Gary D. The Five Love Languages: How to Express Heartfelt Commitment to Your Mate. Chicago: Northfield Pub., 2004. Print.

"DiSC Profile - The DiSC Profile: From William Moulton Marston to Inscape ToWiley." DiSCProfile.com. N.p., n.d. Web

"Dr. Pauline Rose Clance - IMPOSTOR PHENOMENON." Dr. Pauline Rose Clance - IMPOSTOR PHENOMENON. N.p., n.d. Web.

"Facts & Statistics." Anxiety and Depression Association of America, ADAA. N.p., n.d. Web

Gladwell, Malcolm. Outliers: The Story of Success. New York: Little, Brown, 2008. Print

Greenleaf, Robert K. The Servant as Leader. Indianapolis, IN: Robert K. Greenleaf Center, 1991. Print.

Rath, Tom. Strengths Finder 2.0. New York: Gallup, 2007. Print.

Ruane, Isabel. ""Effortless Perfection"." Harvard Magazine. N.p., 03 Mar. 2014. Web

Yao, Amy. "'Never Let Them See You Sweat': The Myth of Effortless Perfection." The Huffington Post. TheHuffingtonPost.com, n.d. Web.

# acknowledgments

A heartfelt thank you to all of my sweet friends and remarkable clients who kept encouraging me to pursue this book of mine.

A special acknowledgment goes to my tight circle of friends - my board of directors, my inspiration, and my reflection. A shout of love goes to Suzanne, Staci, Mary Ann, Ashley, Shannon, and Stephanie. And of course, Erin, Gretchen, Michelle, Jill, Abigail, Jana, and Rosie, as well as my adventure crew Nicole, Leah and Chris. As my parents remind me, "You only have courageous friends. Every last one of them is tough as nails." It's so true. It is a constant joy to have friends who are wickedly smart and fiercely thoughtful.

And for all of the women in the world who are told they are less than, I am lucky to have a guy who thinks the hottest part of my body is my brain. He is the guy who brags to his friends about my success, and loves that my business is growing wildly. Even when he is scared of all of this change, he is the one cheering next to me, and pushing me to grow. So many men are afraid of their partner's success because it may dampen theirs, but I am lucky to have a partner that does just the opposite. He can light up an entire room on his own accord, but he never forgets to let my light shine just as bright.

Finally, a thank you goes to my longtime friend Danielle who has been in charge of so many parts of my business. She has developed an understanding of what is going on in my brain, even when I can't fully explain a new idea, a concept, a graphic, or a layout. She in an invaluable member of my team, and I trust her with so much – including the beautiful layout of this book. Thank you - for everything!

# Notes from Radically Unfinished:

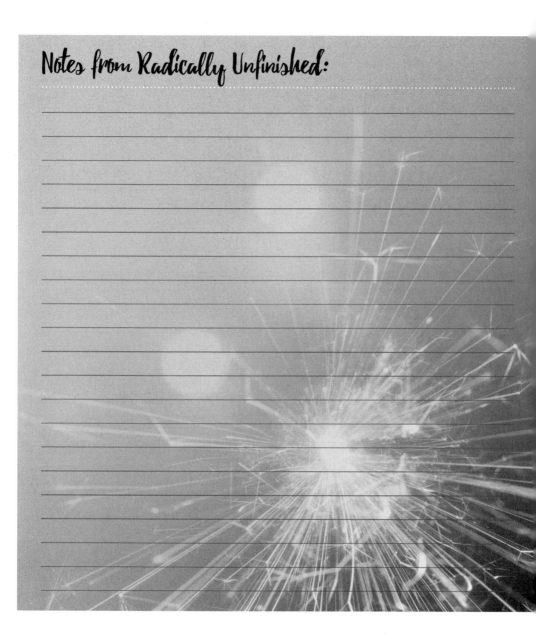

# Notes from Radically Unfinished:

# Notes from Radically Unfinished:

# Notes from Radically Unfinished:

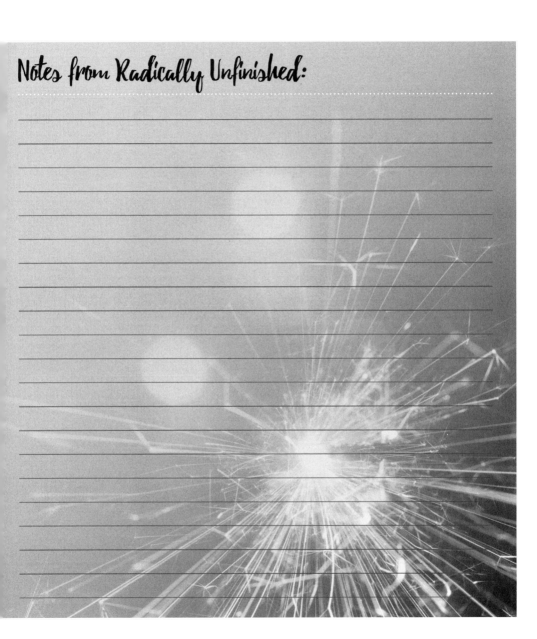

# about erin

**Erin Fischer is the owner and CEO of The Leadership and Training Studio.** She has spoken in 46 states, recruited in Hungary, volunteered in Hawaii, taught in Brazil, and has been on stages with thousands of people in the audience, all with the focus of building teams and organizations.

Erin considers herself a leadership nerd - a woman on a mission to help people excel at what they love to do. Her forum is the stage, but her focus is super-cognitive skills. She wants to support the growth of people by giving them time to think, reflect, and gain new knowledge.

Her favorite topic is confidence for women, but she also speaks on all the human relationship skills – you know, the ones that make great leaders.

So, she thinks, writes, travels, speaks, and reads constantly. You will find her on the road since she is full of wanderlust and craves change and challenge.

Connect with Erin at **www.theleadershipandtrainingstudio.com**